STREETCARS IN THE KOOTENAYS

Cover drawing:

by Susan Gardiner, a long-time member of
Edmonton's art community. The work is
based on a photograph of Baker Street,
Nelson, in the early part of this century.
The original photograph is on page 38.

DOUGLAS V. PARKER

Streetcars in the Kootenays
Nelson's Tramways, 1899 -1992

HAVELOCK HOUSE
Edmonton, Alberta, Canada

Havelock House
5211 Lansdowne Drive
Edmonton, Alberta, Canada
T6H 4L2

Edited by Sheila M. White
Book design by Sheila M. White and Douglas V. Parker

Printed on acid-free paper
Printed in Canada by University of Alberta Printing Services

99 98 97 96 95 94 93 92   6 5 4 3 2 1

Canadian Cataloguing in Publication Data

Parker, Douglas V.
  Streetcars in the Kootenays

  Includes bibliographical references and index.
  ISBN 0-920805-02-7

  1. Street railroads—British Columbia—
Nelson—History. 2. Nelson Electric Tramway
Co.—History. 3. Nelson Street Railway
Company—History. I. Title.
  HE4509.N44P37 1992   388.4'6'0971162   C92-091859-X

iv

To my father, Frank Vernon Parker, who was
thoughtful enough to introduce me to streetcars

CONTENTS

x

MAPS AND DRAWINGS

Acknowledgements

A book such as the present work belongs to the author only up to a point. Many people have been kind enough to share with me their insights, expertise, and photographs from their private collections. I am deeply grateful to each of them.

My earliest contact with those interested in this topic was the late Les Hall, the last superintendent of the Nelson Street Railway. Les patiently answered my many questions, drew maps and sketches to show me where I was in error, and loaned me his treasured photographs. The outcome of all this was the *Nelson Street Railway*, a modest eighteen page document, whose publication introduced me in turn to E.L. (Ted) Affleck, a respected historian of the Kootenay region. After reading my modest history, Ted was kind enough to share some of his early experiences on Nelson's streetcars with me and when he found out many years later that I was engaged on a totally new work on the same topic, he generously allowed me to draw from his own manuscript on the subject. As the writing proceeded, Ted offered additional insights into life in Nelson in the 1930s, finally contributing many helpful comments on the preliminary draft of the manuscript.

I treasure the letters which I received from the late Lyle Ward, letters in which he described the ongoing restoration of #23. My only regret is that neither Lyle nor Les lived to see their beloved streetcar return to service.

Others who were kind enough to read the manuscript included Wilfred Hall and Clara Sutherland (Les Hall's brother and daughter), Robert R. Clark and Dr. Michael Culham (each of whom played a major role in the restoration of a street railway to Nelson in the early 1990s); Brian Kelly and Peter Cox (both respected street railway historians); Carol and Terry Thompson (long-time Nelson residents with a strong interest in street railways), and Gordon White (who generously agreed to read the manuscript from the point of view of the reader who might pick up the book through interest in the area). The last three-named in particular offered many important suggestions for clarifying for the reader those parts of the book which assumed too much background knowledge. To all of these - if the book is a good one, it is the result of your input. If it still lacks clarity or contains errors, the fault is mine.

Dar Churcher of the British Columbia Archives and Records Service and Shawn Lamb of the Nelson Museum went to a great deal of trouble to ensure that the photographic content was the very best. I know that other authors have expressed appreciation for the contribution made to their works by these two women, and I should like in turn to add my thanks. Their photographers, George Piercy in the case of the first-named institution, and Michael Cormie in the case of the second, were painstaking in their preparation of the photos we needed.

Doug Ormond, city administrator of Nelson, kindly provided us with a work area in which to read through the files and other records which he made available to us. With his help we were able to gain a much better sense of the events leading up to the restoration of #23 and the return of streetcar service to the city.

Finally, I would like to express my deep-felt appreciation for the contribution of my editor, Sheila White, who patiently, and always with good humour, brought order into what at times must have seemed a rather chaotic collection of notes. I feel that I have grown as a writer as the result of her patient and thoroughly professional treatment both of me and of my manuscript.

DOUGLAS V. PARKER

PREFACE

Some thirty years ago I wrote the first version of this history of Nelson's street railway systems. At that time, my understanding of street railways was based on my own experiences, largely as a passenger, with the systems in Toronto, where I grew up, and in Winnipeg, where I attended university. Since that first work appeared, however, I have had the privilege of helping to build and operate the street railway system at Fort Edmonton Park. As a result of this first-hand experience, I believe that I have gained a great deal more insight into the problems faced by the men who built, maintained and operated the street railway in Nelson. In presenting *Streetcars in the Kootenays*, therefore, I hope to pay tribute to a group of dedicated men who demonstrated that a small street railway can be every bit as professional an operation as its much larger cousin in the metropolis.

STREETCARS IN THE KOOTENAYS

Part One

1898 to 1949

Introduction

THE PROVINCE OF BRITISH COLUMBIA was unique in
having in its Lower Mainland area Canada's largest
electric railway system, the British Columbia Electric
Railway, and some 120 miles from its eastern boundary, the Nelson Street Railway, which was said at one
time to be the smallest such system in the British
Empire. It would be hard for visitors to the Vancouver
area prior to the 1950s to be unaware of the former
system, for no matter how they arrived in the city, it
would be only a matter of minutes until they encountered one of the BCER's big red and cream cars. On the
other hand, unless their business took them to the
Kootenay region they might be unaware of the Nelson
Street Railway's operations, since Nelson is not located
on the transcontinental route of either of Canada's two
main railway systems. As a result, those responsible for
the operation and maintenance of the smaller system
failed to receive the recognition which they so justly
deserve. For fifty years, from 1899 to 1949, under both
private and public ownership, the cars of the Nelson
Electric Tramway Company and its successors furnished dependable street railway transportation to the
city's inhabitants.

Chapter One

BEFORE THE STREETCARS CAME

Early History of the Nelson Region

THE CITY OF NELSON, BRITISH COLUMBIA, overlooks
the West Arm of Kootenay Lake amidst the natural
grandeur of the Selkirk Mountains. An early settler to
the area, Charles St. Barbe, describes the site and ex-
plains the advantages of its location.

The Arrow lakes, which are part of the Columbia River, lie
about 200 miles west of the Rocky mountains. Down these
beautiful lakes navigation is possible from Revelstoke on the
north to Northport in the state of Washington, a distance of
250 miles. Between the Arrow lakes and the Rockies, and
parallel to both, lies the Kootenay lake embosomed in the
Selkirk ranges which rise in craggy peaks to a height of
10,000 feet. In early days this lake was called Flat Bow lake.
From the west side of Kootenay lake issues its west arm or
outlet navigable for 20 miles to where Nelson now stands.
About a mile below Nelson the outlet becomes a rapid river
falling about 350 feet in its journey of 25 miles to join the
Columbia. Southwards from Nelson ascends a valley, known
as Cottonwood Smith creek (although the Smith is usually
dropped) which communicates by a low pass with the
Salmon river the valley of which leads down to the fertile
plains of Washington and affords facilities for communication with the entire railway system of the United States. In
1893 Mr. Corbin, the president of the Spokane Falls &

KOOTENAY DISTRICT
In general only locations which are referred to in the text have been shown.
not to scale
Golden
to Calgary
Columbia River
Canadian Pacific Railway
Revelstoke
Arrowhead
to Vancouver
Upper Arrow Lake
Lower Columbia Lake
Upper Columbia Lake
Nakusp
Kootenay Lake
Sandon
Kaslo
Kootenay River
Slocan
Lower Arrow Lake
Nelson
Crows Nest Pass Railway (CPR)
Nelson & Fort Sheppard Railway (Great Northern)
Ymir
Columbia & Kootenay Railway (CPR)
Castlegar
Robson
Kushkonook
to Calgary
Trail
Kootenay Landing
Ft. Sheppard
Rykert's
Canada
Northport
Laclede
International Boundary
U.S.A.
Colville
Bonner's Ferry
Columbia River
to Spokane
Kalispell
DVP

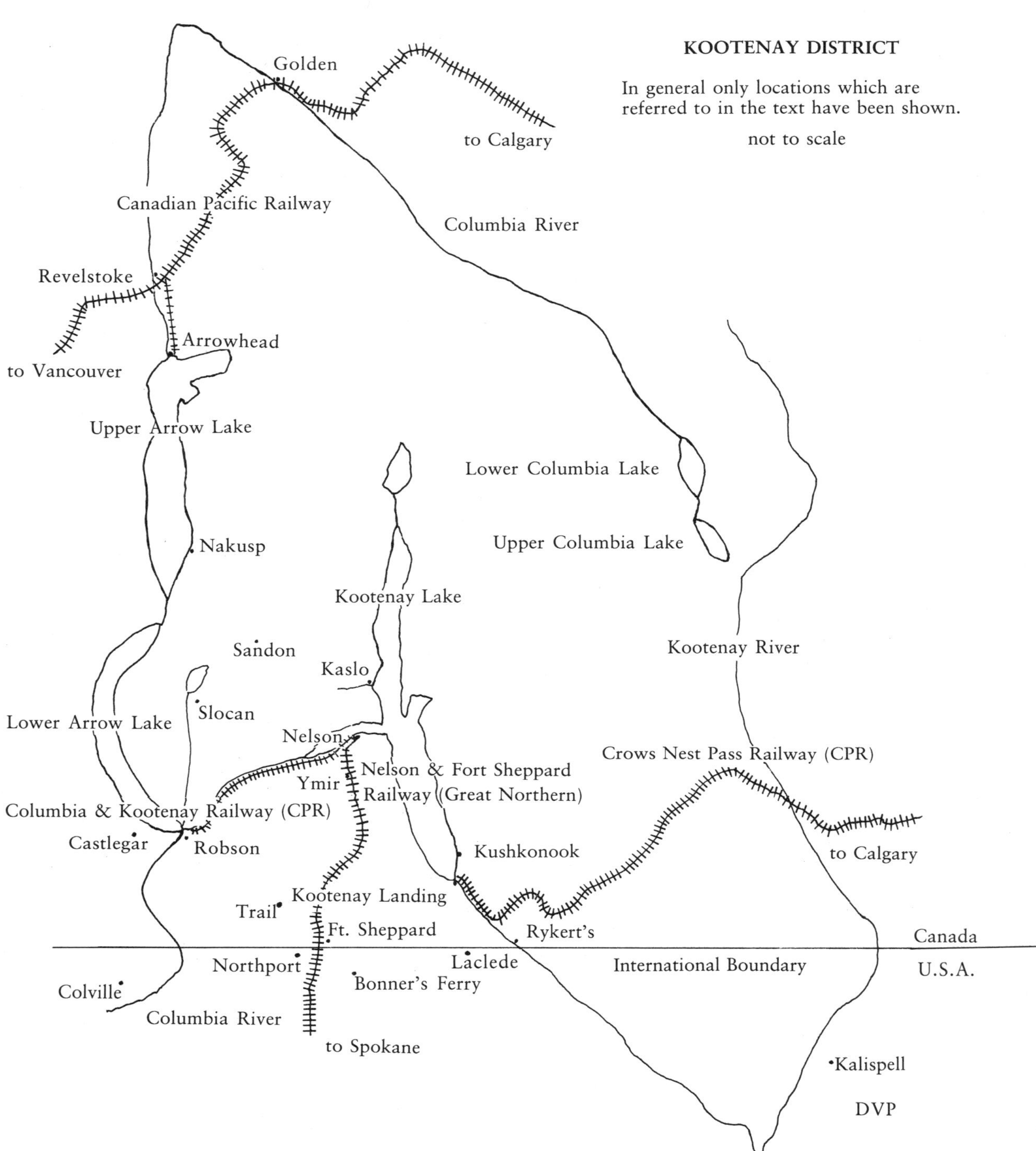

4

Northern railway extended his line under the name of the Nelson and Fort Sheppard railway by this route to Nelson. Before this the Columbia & Kootenay railway had built their line in from Robson on the Columbia river so that Nelson has the unique advantage of perfect water communication with all the magnificient mineral country bordering on the Kootenay lake including the towns of Balfour, Kaslo, Ainsworth, Pilot Bay, Sanca, and last but not least Bonner's Ferry in the state of Idaho, a station on the main line of the Great Northern railway . . .

The actual site of [Nelson] is where the valley of the Cottonwood broadens out and descends in a succession of benches to its junction with the Kootenay river. At the time of the founding of the city these terraces and benches were covered with a dense growth of timber.

An old trapper named Martin Fry who had penetrated the bush for some distance often declared it to be some of the densest in the country.[1]

While Nelson's location later contributed to its importance as a distribution centre, its early prosperity stemmed from the rich mineral deposits for which the region soon became known.* There is a possibility that as early as the 1820s the presence of surface ore was noted on the shores of Kootenay Lake. Some ten years later, Archibald McDonald, in charge of Fort Colville, Washington, brought ore samples back to Colville with him on his return from the Kootenay area. Undoubtedly there were others working there at the same time.

In 1884, Gilbert Sproat, who later played a major role in Nelson's development, was sent by the provincial government to the Kootenay Lake region to examine the mineral potential of the area. While those who sent him probably had gold in mind, Nelson was to owe its success to silver.** In his report, Sproat held that mining prospects for the area were good even though the silver found there was contained in low-grade ore. With improved methods of separating silver from the lead in which it was found, and with the coming of the railways to the region, there was a chance for silver mining to

*One of the legends of the area which St. Barbe reports is that Indians and the early Hudson's Bay men melted down the galena (the common lead ore in which silver is found) to make bullets. He suggests that at the time of the writing of his history there were still remnants of a furnace on the shore near the Blue Bell Mine.

**Gold was in fact discovered at Forty-Nine Mile Creek which flows into the Kootenay River some nine miles below Nelson.

become profitable.

Long before Sproat arrived on the scene, there were settlers and prospectors in the area. One of the earliest was Dick Fry (brother of Martin Fry), the first white man to discover gold in the Pend d'Oreille River. Fry was living on the western shore of Kootenay Lake where he had fled with his Indian wife who had saved him from a massacre. Another was George Wallace Hall who in 1878 pre-empted on the Kootenay Flats, grew wheat, and erected a grist mill to supply flour to the prospectors then working the Kootenay Lake area.

In 1882 a prospector named Robert Sproule, along with three companions, staked the Bluebell Mine some thirty miles from Nelson. His success inevitably brought others to the Kootenay area, among them the Hall brothers, Osmer and Winslow. It may be said that Nelson's history began when the Hall brothers found silver ore on Toad Mountain southeast of the city in 1886.* At that time there were already two men living in log cabins on the lake front at the foot of the mountain, a site now part of the present city. The Hall brothers originally had been looking for gold-bearing sand in the Salmon River. It was the loss of their horses that led them to Toad Mountain and the silver-rich ore.

*Collins offers the following explanation for the name, Toad Mountain. "At the time of the location of the Silver King group no name was given to the mountain upon which the claims were located. The properties were described as being on the divide between Cottonwood Smith and Salmon creeks. The name Toad Mountain was first given on July 27th 1887, when Charlie Townsend and Ben Thomas were staking the Jim Crow, about one and one-half miles from the Silver King group. Townsend was sitting on a log about a foot from the ground writing the location notice. He had proceeded as far as the words 'situate on' when a big warty toad jumped from under the log close by his feet, and seeing it Townsend filled in the words 'Toad Mountain' as the name of the mountain on which the claims were located."[2]

The Silver King Mine in its early stages

Registering their claim at the nearest Canadian land office (located at Donald on the Canadian Pacific Railway) would have required travelling 300 miles through remote and desolate country. They decided instead to rely on the isolation of the area. When the assay on the samples which they had taken out to Colville revealed the enormous value of what they had found, they came back in the spring of 1887 and staked four claims - the American Flag, the Kohinoor, the Kootenay Bonanza, and the Silver King.[3]

Transportation To The Kootenays

From an early date the Kootenays enjoyed excellent communication with the American settlements to the south. The same could not be said for communication lines to the east and to the west within Canada. By 1860, an excellent road had been constructed by the U.S. Army connecting Colville with Wallula, the upstream port on the Columbia River reached by steamers of the Portland-based Oregon Steam Navigation Company. This road enabled many prospectors to leave the steamer at Wallula, travel along the wagon road to Colville, then make their way north to the Big Bend, Forty-Nine Mile Creek, Salmon River, Wild Horse Creek, Kettle River Valley, and other potential mining sites in British Columbia.

The ease with which the Americans could move supplies into Canada from the south along pack trails from Colville, Washington, Laclede, Idaho, and Kalispell, Montana, was not lost on Victoria merchants such as the Rithets who complained bitterly to Governor Seymour. The Governor's response was to ask Edgar Dewdney to look into the possibility of constructing a pack horse trail from Wild Horse (Fisherville) to Similkameen, similar to the trail that Dewdney had built from Hope to Similkameen a few years earlier. In 1865 he set out and eventually reached the Kootenay Lake area where he met Dick Fry.*

Despite the number of prospectors in the field, and the strikes which they undoubtedly made, the development of these mines had to await the introduction of substantial transportation facilities such as railways and steamboats. The economic slump of 1873 effec-

*Here is how Dewdney describes the meeting: "When coming down the west side of the lake, after exploring the northern end, at a point where Ainsworth camp is, we were surprised to find a white man. When we first sighted him he was industriously showing a crowd of Indian children how to shoot with a bow and arrow. He told us his name was Dick Fry... Before leaving he showed me over the hot springs and exhibited several specimens of rich galena float. Fry, with the Hall boys, located the Hall Mine above Nelson."[4]

Nelson, 1891

tively put an end to railway construction until 1881-82 when the Northern Pacific Railway built from Wallula, Washington northeast to Pend d'Oreille Lake and the following year connected with the line extending west from St. Paul, Minnesota. A few years later in 1885, Dr. Wilbur Hendryx, the mining developer, built a wagon road from Kootenai Station, Idaho, on the Northern Pacific to Bonner's Ferry. From that point, steamboats could easily reach Kootenay Lake, opening up the area to further mining development.

The Beginnings of Nelson

After the Hall brothers' find, it was only a matter of months before the upper slopes of Toad Mountain saw the building of some twenty-five cabins. By the winter of 1887-88, between three and four hundred people were living along the banks of Ward Creek in what is now the city of Nelson.

What did this site which eventually became Nelson look like in the late 1880s? A colorful description of it is provided by J.William Cockle. After discussing his purchase of the steam launch *Midge*, he tells of the little vessel's voyage to the site of what is now Nelson.

Midge near Rykert's Landing

The first business offered the *Midge* was to take a party of mining investors headed by one of the Hall boys . . . from Rykert's Landing down to Stanley [one of Nelson's early names].* The trip was uneventful, with the exception of running on to some mud flats along the Outlet, but was made memorable as my first visit to the coming metropolis.

At Stanley we pushed the nose of the *Midge* ashore, or as near ashore as the mud would allow, and disembarked our six passengers, who evinced remarkable agility in negotiating the leaps from rock to rock or the balancing acts required to negotiate the round poles by which some of the intervening spaces were filled. These poles had the bad manners to sink when an undue weight was placed on them, or to slide out sideways when the balance was improperly adjusted by the shifting of a quid from one side to the other; the adhering mud only adding variety to the landscape.

The landing was made about the foot of Hall Street. There faced us as we looked ashore a steep bank on which three or four log shacks had been erected. A climb to the top of the bank and the site of the future metropolis of the Kootenay lay before us. Fire had left nothing of the heavy growth of timber that had previously covered the ground, but a profusion of blackened logs lay everywhere, through which a trail had been cleared from the *steamboat landing* along what is now known as Ward Street.

Adjoining this trail were two tents, the first being occupied as a general store which was owned by Messrs. J. Fred Hume and Bob Lemon. The other tent served as a primitive hotel, under the management of John Ward. It was provided with a stock of both solid and liquid refreshments without which no respectable or self-respecting mining town could ever expect to start business. As everybody packed his own blankets in those days, linen was not furnished with the sleeping accommodations.

A little to the west of this trail near where the provincial jail now stands was a shake shanty occupied by the Spokane mining promotion firm of Dennee, Devine & Co., dealers in everything that a prospector could ask for or desire. It sure was a *bum looking layout* - this vista of future wealth and greatness.[5]

*Harry Anderson, the district's mining recorder and constable, called the area where Nelson now sits Salisbury. However, Gilbert Sproat, the gold commissioner, also carried out a survey and called the area Stanley. Needless to say, this created a certain amount of confusion.

Nelson, 1898, looking toward Toad Mountain from across the Arm

The little settlement grew rapidly, and its inhabitants petitioned Ottawa for a post office, suggesting that the area be called Stanley. Since a post office with that name already existed in the Cariboo, the Federal Government named the new community Nelson in honour of the then lieutenant-governor of the province, Hugh Nelson. An intriguing fact about this early post office is that many of the town's settlers were Americans, and, since United States mail was shipped directly to the U.S. by steamer to Bonner's Ferry, Idaho, the postmaster sold both Canadian and American stamps in the ratio of about two to one.[6]

At about the same time, the adjacent community,

Looking toward Nelson from the smelter site in 1896

then known as *Bogustown*, but now called Fairview, was the scene of some questionable real estate activity. Properties there were being marketed as located in *Nelson City*. While Scott and Hanic[7] suggest the nickname Bogustown derived from this sharp practice, Collins believes it had more to do with the difficulties which men employed there had in getting paid for their labours. As to whether or not the lots were located in Nelson, no one really knew at the time, since Nelson was not incorporated as a city until 1897.[8]

Chapter Two

TRAMWAYS AND PROPOSED TRAMWAYS

Economic Promise

TO ITS EARLY INHABITANTS, Nelson held the promise of becoming a major centre both for shipping and for smelters built to serve the many mines in the area. From Nelson, the port of Robson, situated at the junction of the Kootenay and Columbia rivers, could be reached by trains of the Columbia & Kootenay Railway (leased to the CPR for 999 years). This twenty-five mile line from Nelson to Robson was built in 1891 to bypass the unnavigable sections of the Kootenay River. From Robson, steamers of the Columbia & Kootenay Steam Navigation Company (CKSN) operated downstream to the Spokane Falls & Northern Railway connection at Northport. Other steamers travelled upstream from Robson to Arrowhead and then via the CPR to Revelstoke, providing a connection with the CPR's main line. Still other railways were planned from Nelson to the Crowsnest area with its rich coal deposits, and from Sandon, in the Slocan area, to Kaslo on Kootenay Lake. The Nelson & Fort Sheppard Railway would one day provide a connection with Spokane, the largest U.S. city to the south. The commerce which all this would generate undoubtedly would be translated into jobs for those employed in the construction industry. Nelson's economic future seemed assured.[1]

Proposed Tramways in the Nelson Area

It might be argued that the first street railway-type operation constructed in the Kootenays, albeit on the very edge of the region, was a horse car line. In his book *Come With Me To Yesterday* David Kay describes the tramway system of the Upper Columbia Navigation and Tramway Company incorporated in 1891 ". . . with power to build tramways from Golden station to the steamboat landing on the Columbia river and from Mud (Adela) lake to the north end of Columbia lake." A horse pulled one or two open cars running on light rails. The line's passenger car could seat ten passengers to a side. The steamboat *Pert* picked up the passengers at the end of the tramway and carried them across Columbia Lake. After the trip across the lake, a portage had to be made over the Canal Flats to the Kootenay River, by means of which passengers could reach Fort Steele and points south.[2] The tramway's rails were removed in 1902.[3]

Also in 1891, the provincial legislature passed a statute incorporating the Toad Mountain and Nelson Tramway Company. The act empowered its directors to construct a tramway of single or double track within a radius of six miles from the Silver King Mine, powered "by any motive power," from the mine site on Toad Mountain to "some point on the bank of the Kootenay River at or near Nelson."[4] No work was ever carried out by the line's promoters, and their authority was allowed to lapse.*

*The Toad Mountain and Nelson Tramway Company's charter was repealed during the 1926-27 sitting of the British Columbia legislature.[5]

(In the same year a water company, a fire company, and a telephone system which linked Nelson to other towns around the lake were established. The year 1892 also saw the formation of the Nelson Electric Light Company, even though the new company did not begin supplying electricity for household use until 1896. Almost from the time of its construction, the rapid expansion of the town made the facility inadequate.)

*The men who incorporated this company represented other major enterprises with a stake in the area: Henry Abbott and R.M. Marpole of the Canadian Pacific Railway, D.M. Corbin, an important railway developer from Spokane, and F.J. Barnard, John Irving and J.A. Mara of the Columbia & Kootenay Steam Navigation Company. The company's authority lapsed in 1896 when it failed to complete any of its works by the statutory deadlines.[7]

In April 1892 the Kootenay Power Company* was authorized to "construct, operate, and maintain tramways for the purpose of conveying passengers, freight, and ores from some convenient point near the Town of Nelson to any point or points within a twenty-five mile radius from the said Town of Nelson."[6]

The company was also empowered to build a hydro-electric plant on the Kootenay River and to supply electric power in excess of its street railway requirements to any person within the twenty-five mile radius. Unlike the charter of the Toad Mountain and Nelson Tramway Company which was not too specific about the nature of the proposed line, the charter for the Kootenay Power Company described what was proposed in greater detail.

The company envisaged a street railway linking the Nelson City Wharf at the foot of Hall Street with the Columbia & Kootenay Railway station on Railway Street via Hall, Baker and Railway streets. From Baker and Stanley streets, a branch was to be laid south up Stanley and out Hall Mines Road. The line would then divide, one section climbing Toad Mountain to the community known as Fredericton. A second branch would follow Cottonwood Creek to another community located where Hall Creek and the Salmon River joined, a community which would house those who worked in the Fern Mine and other nearby operations.[8]

Fredericton was a typical mining camp settlement on Toad Mountain. Monty Davys, R.W. Hinton and other mine supervisory personnel settled there with their families. Most of the miners lived in dormitories. Unfortunately, Fredericton held little appeal for families, owing to the amount of snow which fell there, and to the violence typical of such camps. The Fern Mine on Hall Creek Siding also failed to produce a permanent settlement.[9] Consequently, planning for a street railway line far up the side of the mountain came to a halt, and the authority granted to the company lapsed.

The Silver King Mine site 1899

One more charter for a tramway system in the area was granted to the Hall Mines, Limited, operators of the Silver King Mine, the largest such venture in the region, to "... construct tramways and electrical works in the vicinity of Nelson."[9] In addition to roughly the same authority described earlier for the Toad Mountain project with respect to rails, and motive power methods, the Hall Mines firm was empowered to construct power generating facilities to provide electricity for its tramway operation. The tramway system which the company ultimately built was very different from the one described in its charter.

The Hall Mines Company's Aerial Tramway

While the financial panic of 1893 and the flood of 1894 slowed development, the years from 1895 to 1898 were boom times. January, 1896 saw the Hall Mines smelter at Nelson 'blown in', effectively securing jobs for the

16

region as the ore from the Silver King Mines far up Toad Mountain was brought down for processing. Initially *rawhiding* and wagons were used to bring the ore down for shipment elsewhere, since these primitive means could not transport sufficient ore to support a smelter.* The new smelter required large quantities of ore on a daily basis, and to achieve this, the company built an aerial tramway reaching from the mines far up the mountain down to the smelter at its base.

The erection of the tramway was not an easy project.

After many trials and suggestions a wire rope tramway known as the Hallidie system and manufactured by the California Wire Works Co. of San Francisco was decided upon, and Mr. Parsons, the superintendent of the company came in to supervise the erection of the plant. In passing it may be mentioned that the Mr. Hallidie who gave his name

Centre station on the Hall Mines Aerial Tramway

to the system [and also built the first San Francisco cable car system] was not unknown to the Province, as it was he who built the famous suspension bridge across the Fraser on the old Cariboo road. The difficulties Mr. Parsons had to contend with were by no means light. The survey for the tramway showed the distance to be 4 1/2 miles and the height of the mine above the smelter site 4,800 feet. Crossing its line was the canyon of Grosvenor creek necessitating a long span without supports. All of these troubles were overcome and the tramway as erected was the longest in the world upon that system. It acts entirely by gravity, the full buckets descending hauling up the empty ones. But the strain was too great. Four miles and a half of buckets holding one hundred pounds of ore each hauling along a distance of almost a mile in sheer descent was more than ordinary iron could stand, so the tramway was eventually cut in two with a loading station halfway down. Since then it has worked with entire satisfaction bringing down about ten tons an hour with ease.[10]

The discovery of rich mining fields in the Slocan area, twenty miles to the northwest, was a mixed blessing for Nelson. Those of her merchants who opened up branch stores in the new fields prospered, and by reflection so did Nelson. At the same time, Nelson was very closely tied to one commodity, and the slump in the price of silver in 1893 made itself felt in the little town. Despite this momentary set back and the impact of the flood of 1894, the economy rallied beginning in 1895. Encouraged by the improvement in the financial climate, Nelson's citizens began to consider the construction of a street railway system.

Looking down the mountain slope to Nelson from the aerial tramway towers

Chapter Three

THE NELSON ELECTRIC TRAMWAY COMPANY   1898-1908

Boom Times

THE RICH MINERAL DISCOVERIES of the Kootenay
would not be overshadowed by the Klondike gold rush
for some years to come, and for a time the area enjoyed
a renown second only to that of the diamond mines of
the Transvaal. Throughout the 1880s and 90s the spe-
culative mindset which such activity seems to foster,
encouraged countless, though not always soundly-based,
schemes for making money. Discoveries of gold and
silver in the area unlocked the vaults of men of finance
in distant parts of the world, all eager to participate in
the hope of receiving a rich return on their investments.
Many of these ventures required provincial government
approval, but the legislative buildings in Victoria were
a long way off, and perhaps the provincial government
listened more readily to their promoters, than might
have been the case if the proposals had been somewhat
closer at hand. In an atmosphere of such feverish
optimism developers of street railway systems received
their greatest encouragement, and in this, the Nelson
area proved no exception.

Proposals for a Street Railway

By the 1890s street railways were operating in the coastal cities of Victoria, Vancouver, New Westminster, Port Townsend, and Seattle. Since Nelson seemed destined to share in the prosperity of its coastal neighbors, its residents felt the need for a street railway, the current measure of a city's significance. While the decline of silver prices in 1893 slowed much of the development envisaged for the Kootenays, the economy revived in 1895 following a sharp rise in the price of silver.[1] By 1897 three smelters were at work in the Nelson region. Then, in 1898, the West Kootenay Power & Light Company opened its modern hydro-electric plant at Bonnington Falls on the lower Kootenay River, providing with its enormous generating capacity the very electricity which a street railway would require.

A group of local promoters approached the British Electric Traction Company, which owned and operated over forty street railways in Great Britain, Ireland, and various foreign countries (Appendix III), to see if this firm might consider establishing a street railway in Nelson. At the time, British investors were taking a keen interest in the growing province of British Columbia. The enthusiasm of the men from Nelson led by Captain Thomas J. Duncan, the head of Duncan Mines, Limited, (a firm incorporated in England), convinced the giant British corporation that prospects were good for a street railway in this part of the Kootenays.* Soon after, at its July 12, 1898 meeting, Nelson city council read a letter from Charles S. Drummond, who appears to have been involved with both the Duncan Mines Limited and the British Electric Traction Company,[2] in which the latter firm applied for a franchise for a street railway in the city. Drummond's letter reflects the British company's faith in Nelson's future.

The British Electric Traction Co. . . . are desirous of extending their operations to this country, and as Nelson now appears to be in a good position to become large enough to support a street railway line, I have deemed it wise to

*At this time, Rossland was also a thriving centre, and the parent British company considered constructing a street railway there, to be called the Rossland and Sophie Mountain Electric Railway Limited. The plan fell through, possibly because of the decline in mining prospects in the area.[3]

View up to the smelter from the city. Note the Columbia & Kootenay Railway cars at bottom right.

apply to your council for a franchise which would be an inducement to that company to build several miles without delay.

I quite understand that there would be a loss in operations for the first two or possibly three years, but we have considered this, and are prepared to assume it.

The franchise would require to be of such duration as would be an inducement to expend the large sum that would be necessary in this experiment; and I suggest that the time be not less than thirty years . . .

It would require to be a part of the undertaking as from our part of the agreement, that should your city desire to take over the lines and run them, that we should be paid the value of the plant and the business as a going concern, and that such value should be based on an average of years, of say six, three of these years to count back and three forward, to enable us to get at prospective profits, and in that way arrive at a fair estimate of its value as a going concern.

Council was asked to give Mr. Drummond a decision

that evening, as he would be leaving for London the next morning. He was able to carry with him a positive response, as council had supported the concept in the following resolution:

That the City Clerk be authorized to notify Mr. C. S. Drummond, Agent of the British Electric Traction Company, that his Company would be granted a franchise for a Street Railway in this City when terms can be agreed on, and that no unusual restrictions will be asked by the City Council.[4]

Once back in England, Drummond seems to have had little difficulty in persuading his colleagues that the street railway project was viable. On April 24, 1899, council was informed that the British firm had appointed Captain Thomas J. Duncan of the Duncan Mines and Francis W. Peters, the Canadian Pacific Railway's district freight agent, to act as their agents in Nelson and "to organize a company for the purpose of constructing a street railway and operating the same in Nelson as soon as a satisfactory franchise had been granted by the City."[5]

The thirty-year franchise requested by representatives of the proposed company was granted with certain conditions. The parent company was to produce satisfactory evidence that it was financially capable of carrying out the project; the local company would proceed immediately with incorporation under the laws of British Columbia and Canada, and ". . . construction of such railway [was to] be commenced within two months after the incorporation of the company, and be carried on continuously and diligently until completion of at least two (2) miles of railway." For its part, council agreed to submit a by-law to the ratepayers with respect to the contract to be drawn up between the city and the company.[6]

In Nelson, the founders of the proposed street railway were so convinced of their project's future that the British corporation financed its construction entirely from its own funds, offering no public shares whatsoever. As a result, the line was somewhat more stable financially, at least at the outset, than were many similar ventures in North America which depended on subscriptions from local citizens.

In the plebiscite held May 29, 1899, the ratepayers were asked to support By-law No. 42, "A By-law respecting an Electric Street Railway in the City of Nelson." The vote was 249 to 39 in favour, reflecting the high level of public support for the venture. As indicated, the local citizens risked little; they were asked neither to guarantee the company's bonds, nor to buy stock in the enterprise. On the other hand, the city would receive no share of the company's revenues, nor would the company's facilities be either taxed or sub-

Offices of the Nelson Electric Tramway Company at the corner of Josephine and Vernon Streets

jected to municipal licenses for a period of ten years. The by-law was ratified at council's June 5 meeting held the following week.

The franchise which the citizens granted to the company was to last for thirty-five years, at the end of which time the city could, after one year's notice, and upon payment of the actual value of the physical plant, take possession of the system. Should the city elect not to do so, the same option would be open to it every succeeding five years. The city was also given the option of taking over the plant at any point after the first fifteen years of the franchise had elapsed on giving one year's notice. If this option were taken, however, the municipality also had to pay to the company a sum equal to five times the average profits of the past three years' operation. Finally, before beginning construction, the company was asked to deposit two thousand dollars with the city to cover any possible damage which might occur during the laying of the first two miles, an amount which would be returned on completion of this stage.

The city wisely insisted that all poles on graded streets must be painted. Other municipalities had had to contend with overhead poles from which the bark still hung in long tatters. The track was to be standard gauge (4' 8 1/2"), and the crews were to be in uniform. Cars were to stop on the near side of every cross street to take up and let down passengers and were to begin running on all routes not later than 6:30 a.m. Service was to continue until 11:00 p.m. daily with at least fifteen round trips on each route. When a census showed that the population of the city had reached 12,000 - it was 5273 in 1901 - the company and the city engineer with the approval of council would determine what changes might be needed in the frequency of service. Should the company through its own fault fail to operate the cars for a period of two months in any one year, its franchise would be forfeited. Section three of the by-law outlined the proposed fare structure under which the cash fare for adults was to be ten cents with tickets available at the rate of twelve for one dollar. (The detailed fare

The West Kootenay Power & Light Company's power plant (foreground) faces the city-owned facility at Bonnington Falls on the Kootenay River

structure is included in the notes.)[7]

Section 19 of the by-law was to have a severe impact on the company's financial situation. The city owned its own power plant having purchased the Nelson Electric Light Company referred to in the previous chapter. Section 19 states: "Nothing in this By-Law shall be construed as giving the applicants any rights to utilize or dispose of power for any purpose than the operation of their railway or incidental thereto, or to permit any person or corporation supplying them with power to have any such rights." The inclusion of this section ensured that the city-owned plant would never face competition from the West Kootenay company.

Planning began immediately, and by July 25, 1899 Halifax Hall, formerly a Canadian Pacific Railway civil engineer and now the engineer for the tramway company, was able to present city council with a proposed route for the street railway. The main line would run from the Columbia and Kootenay Railway station located at the foot of Railway Street, along Baker to Josephine Street, down Josephine (where a passing track would be located)* to Vernon, and along Vernon to Ward. From Ward Street it would continue along Front Street and Water Street (both now part of Front Street) to the city limits at Poplar Street, passing the Government Wharf at the foot of Hall Street on the way. A few hundred feet east of the city limits was the Nelson & Fort Sheppard Railway station. Another route would start from Stanley and Baker streets, running up Stanley as far as [Hall] Mines Road and along Mines Road to Kootenay which it would ascend as far as Houston. The line would then run along Houston to a point about halfway between Stanley and Ward streets near the Crystal Ice Rink located at Stanley and Houston in what was known as the Hoover Addition. The system would comprise exactly two miles of track and "would connect the principal outlying portions of the city with Baker Street, the Wharf, and the CPR depot."[8] The line, except for the passing track on Josephine Street (later relocated to Hall and Front streets), would be single track throughout, and remain so to the end of operations in 1949. In the outlying areas, much of it would be laid at the side of the road rather than down the middle. At the first spike ceremony held some time later, Drummond suggested that the line might even go as far as the Nelson & Fort Sheppard's Mountain Station located high above Nelson near South Cherry and Gore streets.

The completed line differed somewhat from the description just given. The line's northern end originally was to be at the city limits at Poplar Street (August 1). On August 27, the *NDM* reported that the intention was to extend the line to Bogustown "later on." On November 22, however, the same paper reports that the street railway's track has been laid as far as the Grove Hotel "nearly opposite the Nelson & Fort Sheppard depot." The Grove Hotel was located at the corner of First and Cottonwood streets, and was patronized by travellers using the railway. The tramway's first sched-

*A passing track is used on a single track line to allow two cars travelling in opposite directions to pass.

ule issued January 4, 1900 shows the line running between the Sherbrooke Hotel at Baker and Railway streets (close to the Columbia and Kootenay Railway station) and the Nelson & Fort Sheppard depot. This suggests that track was laid to Cottonwood and First streets instead of just to the city limits.

The Start of Construction

The by-law specified that a contract was to be drawn up between the city and the company, but so impatient was the latter to begin work that at the meeting of council referred to earlier, it asked for permission to make an immediate start without waiting either for provincial acceptance of its registration under the *Tramway Company Incorporation Act* or for its contract with the city to be signed. Permission was granted, and the company scheduled an elaborate *first spike* ceremony for 5:30 p.m., Monday, July 31.

The event took place at the corner of Front and Hall streets. While the band from the Hall Mines smelter played, Charles S. Drummond, representing the British parent company, looked around for someone to hold the spike while he drove it in. Since local citizens had not had a previous opportunity of assessing Mr. Drummond's skill with a spike maul, no one was prepared to risk his fingers! Fortunately, Halifax Hall had foreseen the problem, and when no one volunteered, Drummond drove the spike into a prepared hole. Mayor Neelands then extracted the spike and presented it to Drummond as a memento of the occasion.* Afterward, everyone adjourned to a formal banquet at the Phair Hotel.

The new company was incorporated under the terms of the Province's *Tramway Incorporation Act* on October 4, 1899. In addition to C.S. Drummond, the parent company was represented on the board of directors by E. Garcke, also of London. The local directors, who, Drummond said at the spike-driving ceremony, would have responsibility for determining future extensions,

*The spike, made of silver, copper, and gold, was engraved on its four sides as follows: (i) First spike used in construction, Nelson Electric Tramway; (ii) Driven by Mr. C.S. Drummond, British Traction Tramway Co., Nelson B.C. July 31, 1899; (iii) Presented by His Worship, Mayor Neelands; (iv) The Pioneer Street Railway of the Kootenays.[9]

included Captain T.J. Duncan, J. Laing-Stocks (both of Duncan Mines), F.W. Peters (the popular CPR district freight agent), and W.A. Macdonald, Q.C. At the first meeting of the directors held on October 10, Peters was elected president, T.J. Duncan vice-president, and T.C. Duncan (son of T.J. Duncan) secretary-treasurer. M.F. Carey was appointed electrical superintendent.

The same meeting authorized an order for two double-truck, double-end, closed cars with 21-foot bodies* from the Canadian General Electric Company of Peterborough, Ontario along with all the other necessary electrical components for the system including a motor-generator set. At that time (between 1896 and approximately 1915), Canadian General Electric manufactured not only the electrical equipment, but also the cars themselves.[10] A substation would be built at the western boundary of the city, and company offices established in the Macdonald Block at the corner of Josephine and Vernon Streets.

An interesting fact with respect to the Nelson cars is that Canadian General Electric's records show that the two cars with 21-foot closed bodies, were actually ordered early in August 1899.

Each double-truck car would have four 40-horsepower motors (somewhat more powerful than was usual for that era). Ordinarily streetcars are not expected to climb hills greater than six per cent, i.e., a rise of six feet for every one hundred feet of track, but the grade up Toad Mountain could be as steep as twelve per cent. This situation required somewhat heavier electrical equipment and different gearing. (The reader is referred to the photograph on page 72 which will better illustrate the steepness of the grade.) Conductors would collect fares in a hand-held farebox, ringing up each payment on the fare register installed in each car.** The cars were to be painted a rich claret red picked out with vermilion. Twenty-four passengers could be seated on the red plush seats.

*While a 21-foot body may seem very short to knowledgeable readers, this is the dimension given on the order form. There were, in fact, double-truck cars manufactured elsewhere in the same era even shorter than this.

FIG. 8.—STATIONARY REGISTER.

A typical fare register of the period

**A fare register was provided on each car as a method of auditing. When the conductor collected a fare, he pulled a rope which increased the count of fares in the register by one. At the end of his shift, the cash in his farebox had to tally with the number of fares shown on the register.

28

As an outcome of the same meeting, tenders were called for the construction of a carbarn on a piece of land on the south side of A.B. Shannon's house on Mines Road. Tracks would be laid from the Crystal Rink west on Houston Street to Kootenay Street, then north down the Kootenay Street Hill to Mines Road, east on Mines Road to Stanley Street, then north down Stanley Street to Baker Street. On Baker Street the tracks would run two blocks east to Josephine Street where a passing siding would be laid between Baker and Vernon streets. The track would then run west one block on Vernon Street, then north and east on Front and its eastern extension (then called Water Street) to Poplar Street. Forty-five-pound rail was to be laid on level sections and 60-pound rail on the hills.*11

Politics and Electric Power

Power for the cars was to be supplied not by the city-owned plant, but by the West Kootenay Power and Light Company (WKP&L) of Rossland from their newly-

A British Columbia Electric Railway conductor collects a passenger's fare in a *coffee pot* farebox.

29

The Nelson Electric Tramway Company 1898 to 1908

Based on maps by Les and Wilfred Hall as well as information from other sources

not to scale

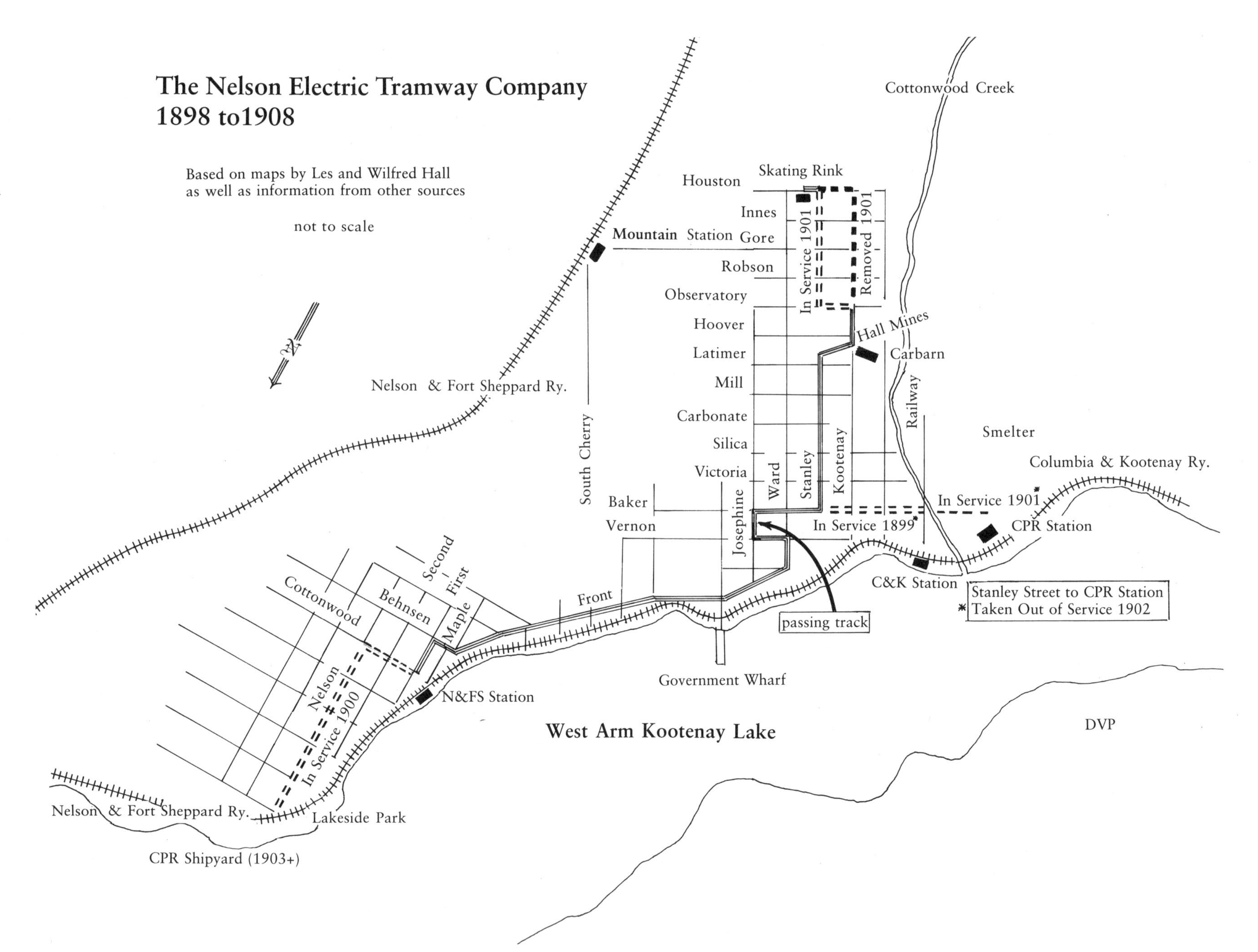

opened Bonnington Falls Plant on the Kootenay River. The WKP&L was to build a transmission line to the street railway's substation where a 500-horsepower, three-phase, revolving field synchronous motor would drive a 325-kilowatt railway generator. Since Nelson had enjoyed electric power since 1896 from the now city-owned plant on Cottonwood Creek, it might be asked why the tramway company did not take its power from this source. To understand why this was not possibile, it will be necessary to go back to 1892 when the Nelson Electric Light Company was incorporated.[12]

The petitioners for its incorporation included Frank S. Barnard, who later played a leading role in the history of the street railway systems in Vancouver and Victoria; John Houston,* at that time editor of the *The Miner,* and six other gentlemen.[13] The new electric company received permission to divert up to two hundred inches** of water from Cottonwood Creek for their pioneer hydro-electric plant. Supply of power from this source soon proved inadequate, since, as Scott and Hanic suggest in their history of Nelson, "From the time the snow melted till mid June, it [Cottonwood Creek] could be a raging cataract; but at all other times of the year it was just a creek."[14] This meant that during part of the year there was barely enough power for lighting purposes, let alone for running a street railway. What was worse, the same act which incorporated Houston's electric company stressed that the electric company's demands were to take into account the prior claim of the Nelson Sawmill Company for water from the same source. Water pressure for the generators came from a wooden dam built across Cottonwood Creek at Observatory Street where the present Rosemont Bridge is located. The little facility could not keep up with the demand and closed in 1908.

Given Mayor Houston's almost fanatic opposition to the West Kootenay Power and Light Company, it was perhaps unfortunate for the tramway company, both financially and politically, that it had entered into an agreement with this firm. The latter had to build a

*Before coming to Nelson, John Houston had been the publisher of a newspaper at Donald. On June 21, 1890 he published the first newspaper in Nelson, *The Miner.* After selling *The Miner,* he established *The Tribune.* Houston tended to identify with the working people of the area rather than with the establishment.

While his participation in the formation of the Nelson Electric Company reflected his desire to provide Nelson's citizens with the utilities they needed, his decision, once he became mayor in 1897, to have the city purchase the company seems as questionable now as it did then. The plebiscite by which this came about was passed by only a few votes, and then only after Houston demanded a recount. In later years, one of the officials present acknowledged that ballots were tampered with during the recount.[15]

Throughout his terms of office, Houston remained fiercely protective of the power company, often to the detriment of both Nelson's citizens and the tramway company.

**An *inch,* or more appropriately, a *miner's inch,* is defined by the *Oxford English Dictionary (1933)* as "That amount of water that will pass in 24 hours through an opening of 1 square inch under a constant pressure of 6 inches."

transmission line to Nelson to meet the street railway's needs, thereby incurring certain fixed costs which the tramway company had to assume by agreeing to purchase an amount of power considerably above its requirements. The street railway may have hoped to sell its unused power to the city. Mayor Houston, however, looked unfavorably on the West Kootenay Power and Light Company (possibly because of his interest in the city-owned plant). It was fortunate for the street railway that he had been unseated as mayor in the civic elections of January 10, 1899. Had he been mayor, he would not have allowed the tramway company to enter into the West Kootenay agreement. To the dismay of the tramway company, when he was re-elected in January 1900, he refused to permit the sale of tramway power (i.e., from the WKP&L) to Nelson industries, since this would be in competition with what he undoubtedly continued to see as his own enterprise. Houston's decision was to have a damaging effect on the future financial position of the tramway.

Nor was electricity the only problem with which the new street railway company had to cope. The second difficulty, however, was of its own making. In the early stages of construction, the tramway company had enjoyed considerable public popularity, which it then jeopardized. Wagoneers had long enjoyed easy access to the Nelson & Fort Sheppard Railway in Bogustown, but when the tramway company purchased land in the area, it notified city council on November 6, 1899 that it proposed to close the road leading to the Nelson & Fort Sheppard facilities unless the city purchased a right of way from the tramway line. "For a few tense days, freight deliveries to and from the Nelson & Fort Sheppard Railway were diverted to the city wharf, then shipped on the Kootenay Railway & Navigation Company steamer *International* which made the connection with the railway upstream at Five Mile Point. Passengers simply braved the trail to the railway's Mountain Station* perched on the heights near South Cherry and Gore streets."[16] The company eventually realized its mistake and re-opened the road to the public, but not

John Houston, Nelson's first mayor

*The N&FS's Mountain Station was located at an elevation of some 200 feet above the same railway's terminal on the lakefront in Nelson. Trains arriving at Mountain Station from the United States border descended to water level at Troup Junction located at Five Mile Point (five miles from Nelson), reversed, then followed the lakeshore into the city.

before it had lost a great deal of public goodwill.

By November 2, 1899, the track was complete except for the section on Baker Street from Stanley to the Columbia and Kootenay Railway depot on Railway Street. This section was completed by the end of the month. The poles were all in place, men were stringing the wires, and the power line from Bonnington Falls was within two and one half miles of the city. The machinery to be used temporarily for the power supply arrived November 1, and was being installed.[17]

The first car for the new system arrived in Nelson on November 21, 1899 after a trip over the CPR's new Crowsnest Pass route. Since it would be some years yet before the CPR's rails reached Nelson from Kootenay Landing, the car was barged down the lake from the landing on a flat car.[18] For a time it was stored under canvas on a siding near the Sampling Works where it was joined a week later by the second car. A temporary track was laid between the Columbia & Kootenay's line and that of the tramway near Front and Hall streets. On December 11 the two cars were moved onto their own rails and stored in the open at Water Street just inside the city limits until the street railway was ready for operation. On Wednesday, December 12, they made a trial run.

Service Begins

Service was to begin officially the next day, but now the first of a series of incidents which plagued the infant operation took place. As soon as the power was turned on, a motor burned out in the temporary generating equipment. By Thursday, December 21 repairs had been completed, and the first car ventured onto the main line.

Under the headline "FIRST TRAMCAR", the *Nelson Daily Miner* described the event in its December twenty-second issue.

Yesterday was a red letter day in Nelson. The first electric tram car run in the Kootenays passed through the streets of the Inland Capital on that occasion. As already announced it was the intention of the management to have had the service established a week ago but an accident at the power house altered the programme. However it was decided to run no risks and not to turn on the power until everything was proved to be in thorough working order. This happy stage was reached yesterday. Power was turned on shortly after 2 o'clock and a few minutes later the first electric car that has ever run in the Kootenays started from the east end of the service just within the City Limits. Mr. L.A. [Lorne] Campbell, the general manager of the Company [actually of the West Kootenay Power & Light Company] and an electrician of great experience took charge of the motor, Conductor Leicester taking his place on the rear platform and attending the life line [probably the rope communicating with the motorman's bell] and business gong [the fare register which had a bell to signal the passenger that his or her fare had been recorded]. On board the car were: F.W. Peters, president of the Company, Captain Duncan, H.E. Beasley, Mayor Neelands, Ald. Fletcher, Ald. Hillyer, Halifax Hall (the Company's engineer) and several others. The object was to test the plant. The first car to start was No. 2 painted a bright red and bearing the name of the Nelson [Electric] Tramway Co. in conspicuous letters on both sides . . .

As the welcome jingle of the gong was heard everybody along the route turned out to witness the agreeable innovation and although there was no cheering all were evidently delighted to realize that Nelson had taken the lead in this as in other enterprises. No. 2 worked along steadily over the rails to the west end of Baker Street [probably to the Columbia & Kootenay Railroad station] where a halt was made and reversing the line the car was turned on the homeward trip. All worked most satisfactorily and the car was duly christened the Duncan Limited.

As soon as No. 2 had been pronounced well and truly tried No. 1 was given its initial trip and was voted the equal of its successor in every way. While the first car was not brought up the steep grade at Stanley Street the second (#1) was run over this piece of difficult ground and behaved well. The brakes were not plied until the car reached its destination the power station. After a few minutes' pause here the down-grade was attacked on the return journey and although the rails were as slippery as could be imagined in consequence of the lodged snow all worked smoothly . . .

The horses of Nelson took very kindly to the tramcars none of them shying as the novel looking vehicles approached or appearing to notice the ringing of the gong. Not so with the canine species. The dogs displayed considerable uneasiness as the cars passed along and not a few of them had narrow escapes from being electrocuted or run over.

Tragedy

Despite this promising beginning, a second misfortune marred the opening of the new line, this one of a more serious nature than a burned-out generator. The management had intended to inaugurate service shortly after 1:00 p.m., Saturday, December 23, 1899. Through a most fortunate decision on someone's part, it was

One of Nelson's first streetcars on Baker Street

35

decided to have the crews make a few trips over the line before noon in order to help them gain more experience, and in order to test everything thoroughly. The first training trip using #2 went well. On the second trip the car reached the Kootenay Street end of the line without difficulty. On board were the street railway's electrical engineer, M.F. Carey; two motormen, M.T. Peters and Edward Wilson; and two conductors, James Hawkins and William Campion, together with T.C. Duncan, secretary of the company. On the trip up the hill Peters acted as motorman, then turned the controls over to Wilson for the trip back down the steep grade on Kootenay Street. It should be noted that the cars were equipped only with handbrakes; air brakes had not been specified in the original contract.

Several of those on board later testified that part way down the hill Carey warned Wilson that he was driving too quickly. Peters took the controls from Wilson in a

A sample of the Nelson Electric Tramway Company's letterhead

The Nelson Electric Tramway Co., Ltd.

Telegraphic Address:
    " Drumbrough, Nelson, B. C."

P. O. Drawer R.

NELSON, B.C.,   Jan. 29th. 1900.

West Kootenay Power & Light Co.

Rossland, B. C.

Dear Sirs:-

I enclose herewith cheque for $22.20 in settlement of enclosed account of the Western Electric Co., which please return to me receipted.

Yours truly

T. C. Duncan

Secretary

futile last-minute attempt to stop the car. However, by the time the car reached the curve at Hall Mines Road, it was moving so quickly that it failed to make the turn and derailed, falling on its side in the process. Four of those on board jumped before the car overturned some six feet from the track, but Peters was jammed under the car for several minutes before spectators were able to pry the car up and extricate him. He was taken to hospital where his arm had to be amputated. Mr. Duncan stayed with the car as well, but not being on the front platform he escaped with only a shaking up. The four others who jumped, including Wilson, escaped with cuts and bruises. Peters sued the company but was unable to prove negligence, since Carey had warned Wilson that he was driving too fast.[19] Peters subsequently returned to his home in Spokane, while Wilson continued to work as a car cleaner.

In spite of this unfortunate beginning, regular service began with one car in operation on Wednesday, December 27, 1899, running from the Nelson & Fort Sheppard station in Bogustown to Baker and Stanley streets. The service was well patronized despite the accident. It was February, 1900, however, before the other car returned to service, having sustained approximately $200 damage in the accident. (As a comparison, in 1899 the monthly salary for the street railway superintendent in a city such as Victoria was $200, its chief engineer $100, and an inspector $70.[20]) Operation of cars on Stanley Street had to be postponed until more effective hand brakes and the motor-generator set arrived.

By January 4, 1900, the new company was ready to provide its first public timetable. The cars would connect with each arriving train and steamer, and in the process complete the round trip from the Sherbrooke Hotel at the corner of Railway Street and Baker to the Nelson and Fort Sheppard Railway depot every half hour. The first car left the Sherbrooke at 7 a.m. and the N. & F.S. depot at 7:15, leaving the Sherbrooke again at 7:30 a.m. and so on throughout the day. The last car would start at 9:45 p.m.[21]

While other companies faced a 'no cars on Sunday' problem, the Nelson Electric Tramway Company was not similarly restricted. Introduction of Sunday street-car service in the late 1800s in most Canadian cities outside Quebec had been marked by bitter opposition from the churches. As early as 1861, the franchise granted to the Toronto Street Railway Company stated that, "No [horse]car shall run on Sunday."[22] Similar struggles took place in Hamilton, Winnipeg, and Calgary. Toronto's citizens finally accepted Sunday service in 1897 following a plebiscite which passed, 16372 to 16051, a scant 321 vote majority.[23] In Toronto's suburb of Mimico, it was 1901 before such authority was granted.[24]

N.E.T. Co. car #3 on Baker Street

The fact that Sunday operation presented no apparent difficulties in Nelson may have reflected the attitude in Victoria and Vancouver. In fact, the first full day of operation in Victoria took place on Sunday, February 23, 1890.[25] By the time Nelson began operation, the battle was all but over. Under the terms of the by-law incorporating the street railway, there was no restriction. The company simply ran a car on Sunday; if there were complaints, there is no formal record of them. Not long after the operation began, a Salvation Army band even climbed on board one car and provided a musical interlude out to the end of the line.

Almost immediately there were improvements. At the end of January the *Nelson Daily Miner** announced that electric heaters were being installed in the cars.[26] There were losses, too. In February, 1900, C. Halifax Hall left the company's employment to be replaced by M.E. Carey, whose duties were expanded to include all aspects of the company's operations. Although Carey took over at a time when the British public began to be somewhat wary of overseas investments, probably because of endless bad news from South Africa where British troops were fighting in the Boer War, this did not appreciably affect the tramway's plans for expansion.

Service Expands

With the coming of warm weather, the tramway company considered the possibility of generating additional revenue from citizens in search of relaxation. For the time being, however, its tracks stopped near the corner of Cottonwood and First streets in Bogustown, and, according to Scott and Hanic, this in itself may have accounted for much of the revenue in those first months. As the two authors write, "Here, on what is now the quiet corner of Cottonwood and First streets, once flourished a large edifice surrounded by beer gardens, which on summer nights were lit by lanterns casting an enticing glow."[27] This *edifice* was the Grove Hotel, originally built for the convenience of travellers on the Nelson & Fort Sheppard Railway. In addition to the facilities just mentioned, it held the added attraction of being located in Bogustown just outside the city limits, and so beyond the jurisdiction of the local police. The hostelry remained an undoubted source of revenue for the tramway company, even after the Nelson & Fort Sheppard station closed on January 1, 1901.

In an effort to establish an attraction more suited to family outings, the street railway considered building a two and one half mile extension to Florence Park, located at Three Mile (also known as Bealby's) Point, but the capital outlay was calculated to be more than the revenues which the new facility might generate.[28] It was decided instead to extend the line to the foot of Nelson Avenue close to the company's new park in Bogustown (an area later given the more refined name of Fairview) where a bandstand was built, with the promise of boathouses and bathhouses at a later date. Provision was also to be made for athletic grounds for baseball, cricket, and lacrosse.[29] All were to be located on land leased by the street railway, namely the site of the former turning wye used by the Nelson and Fort Sheppard trains until 1897 when the new rail connection was laid along the waterfront to the facilities of the Columbia and Kootenay Railway.

Although work on the street railway's extension to the park was not finished, the company opened its new facility, originally called Lake Park but later Lakeside Park (and Tramway Park in at least one older photograph), on Saturday, June 2, 1900. Two weeks later a dance pavilion opened in the same location ensuring, at least on weekends, a substantial traffic from this part of the system, since an extra car was usually laid on to take the dancers home after the festivities. The bandstand itself was the scene of many memorable concerts provided by the band of the Rocky Mountain Rangers, a local militia regiment.

Perhaps as a means of stimulating revenue from visitors to the new park, the management, early in November 1899, ordered a 21-foot, open car from Canadian

General Electric.[30] The car that arrived was actually much longer and was of a type known as the *Duplex Car* built under licence from the Duplex Car Company of New York by the Briggs Carriage Company of Amesbury Massachusetts.* It is possible that the Canadian General Electric Company either acted as a middleman in its acquisition or had taken it as a trade on other equipment. The car was painted yellow - a very different colour scheme from the other two cars. It arrived February 29, 1900, and, judging by the photograph of it with its load of happy passengers shown on page 43 was undoubtedly a popular addition to the system. The new car was placed in service about 4:30 p.m., Saturday, May 5, 1900, and was well patronized despite inclement weather that day.

There were other changes about to take place. The *NDM* of April 8, 1900 mentions that the motor-generator had arrived in Nelson and would take roughly two weeks to install. The following day saw the re-opening of service up the hill to the skating rink

*The Briggs Carriage Company had been manufacturers of carriages and wagons for many years prior to their entry into the street railway field. In 1903, the company was taken over by the Southern Car Company of High Point, North Carolina, and later produced automobile bodies.

The Duplex Car was a convertible car in that the sides in summer could be rolled up into the roof which accounts for the curve on the pillars as well as the grooves along which the sections ran when being pushed up or pulled down. Maintenance was found to be difficult which may account for the small numbers built. Another manufacturer of these cars was the firm of Jackson and Sharpe of Wilmington, Delaware.[31]

Lakeside Park after the arrival of the automobile

terminus, a service which had been closed since the accident. Since many Nelson residents were understandably apprehensive about this part of the line, the company emphasized that all cars had now been equipped with governors to check excessive speed.

The line to Lakeside Park was finally completed on July 1, 1900, even though the park's formal opening had already taken place on June 2. In the interval, since overhead wires had not yet been strung on the Nelson Avenue extension to Lakeside Park, passengers for that destination presumably still had to walk a short distance. The Nelson City Band, hired by the tramway company, offered Saturday night and Sunday afternoon band concerts, while the dance pavilion proved to be very popular with the younger set. So keen was the street railway to entice customers to the site that it even provided a special after-hours car to the uphill end of the system.[32]

Although the photograph of #3 on page 43 shows the car decorated for an Empire Day ceremony, both passengers and car were probably decorated in a similar fashion for the visit of the Governor General, the Earl of Minto, on September 12, 1900. The Columbia & Kootenay Railway brought Lord Minto and his party to Nelson from Robson. They were taken by carriage to the Central School Grounds at Mill and Stanley streets,

The *Moyie* is one of two Canadian Pacific stern paddlewheelers still preserved. It is undergoing restoration at Kaslo, B.C., where it is open to the public. The other is the *Sicamous*, preserved at Penticton, B.C.

where Nelson's school children were waiting to sing patriotic songs, as was the custom in Canada for many years. Afterward, Lord Minto's party boarded #3 for a ride to Lakeside Park, then returned to the City Wharf for a short trip up the West Arm on board the much-decorated CPR sternwheeler *Moyie*. That evening the vice-regal party attended a public reception at the Phair Hotel, after which the *Moyie* carried them to Kootenay Landing and a waiting eastbound train.[33]

More Problems

That fall, the tramway company lost many of those who had started it on its way. The first to leave was Captain Duncan, who, with his wife, retired to live in San Francisco. In November, Duncan's son resigned as manager and secretary-treasurer. The British Electric

Car 3 decorated for an Empire Day celebration

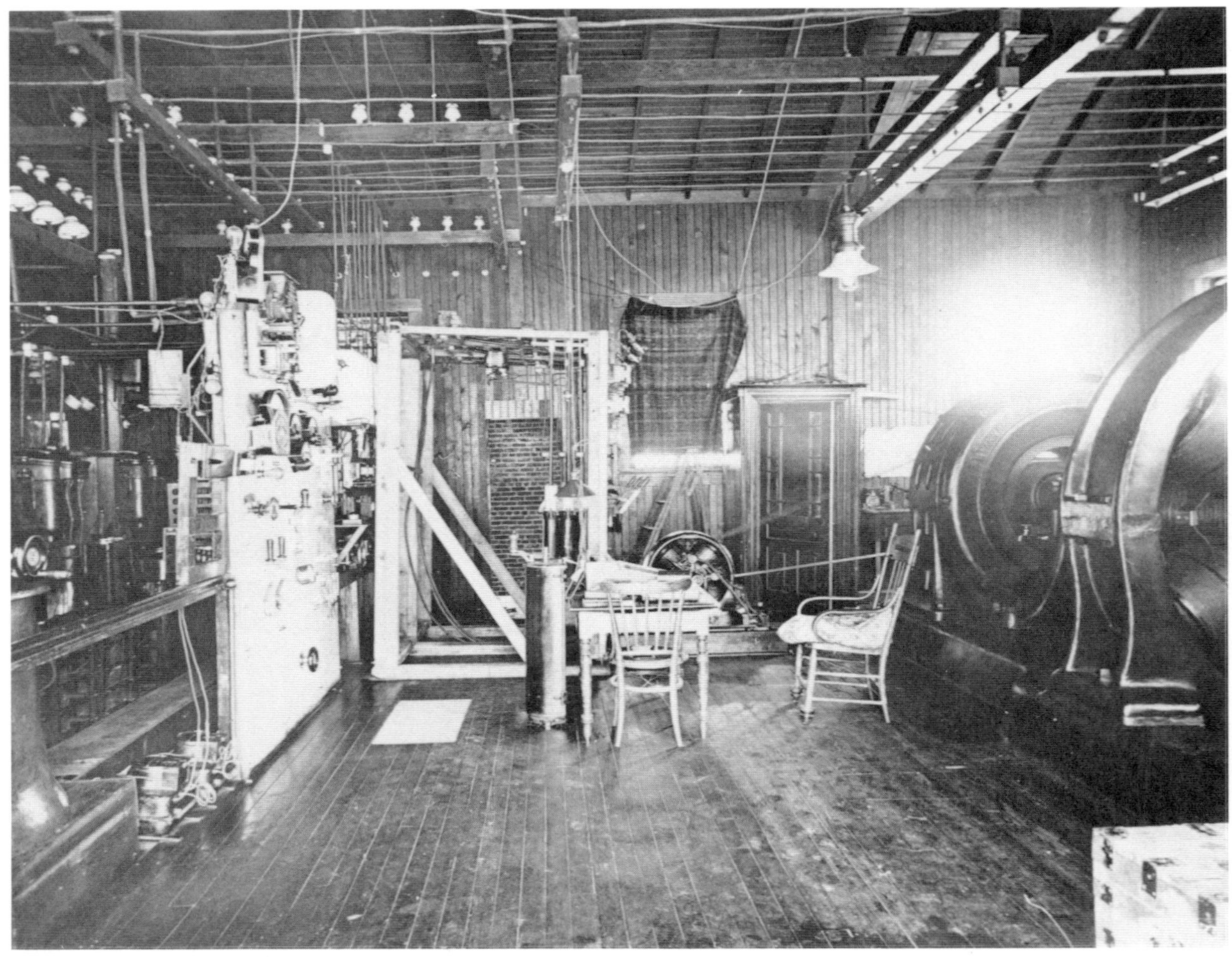

An interior view of the N.E.T. Co.'s electrical substation showing the motor-generator at the right side of the photograph

Traction Company sent A.V. Mason in his place and transferred Superintendent Carey to Auckland, New Zealand. Finally, Nelson residents witnessed the departure of President Francis W. Peters, a popular member of the community, who was transferred by his employers, the Canadian Pacific Railway, to Vancouver. He was succeeded by Henry E. Croasdaile who had held a senior post in the Silver King Mine.[34] Croasdaile acted as president until at least 1908.

The loss of these founding members came at a difficult time in the company's history. The reader may recall the earlier discussion with respect to the negotiations for the supply of electrical power between the tramway company and the West Kootenay Power &

Light Company. The street railway had intended to sell its surplus power to other Nelson businesses, a practice which, under Mayor Neelands, would have encountered no opposition. Unfortunately, John Houston, a vigorous opponent of the West Kootenay company, was returned as mayor in the 1900 elections. No sooner was Houston back than he began identifying instances where West Kootenay power was being sold to Nelson business firms by the street railway. Before long he discovered that Burns and Company, the meat packers, proposed to run their refrigeration plant on West Kootenay power. Houston attempted to deliver a thorough dressing down to Burns' local manager, Alderman Blake Wilson. Wilson, however, reminded the mayor of the many problems caused by the inadequate power supply from the city-owned plant on Cottonwood Creek. If the mayor wished to restrict Wilson's company to city power, then, the alderman hinted, Burns might have to move its plant elsewhere.[35]

Caught in a desperate financial position, the street railway took two steps. Effective November 10, 1900, it reduced its schedule to single car service, stating that this would continue until it could dispose of some of its surplus power. The company had hoped to continue the two-car service throughout the winter and to reduce the fare to five cents, but this was conditional on its being able to sell the power for which it was obliged to pay, but unable to use. Earlier, on October 24th, in an attempt to solve the problem, the tramway company had approached the city's board of works and offered to take over street lighting at a lower cost than if the city were to build a steam plant to meet the increasing demand for electricity in Nelson. The board of works accepted the offer, but Mayor Houston steadfastly refused to consider any offer from the tramway which involved West Kootenay power.[36]

While attempting to deal with the intransigent attitude of the mayor, the tramway company was attacked on another front. During construction of its track in the last months of 1899, the street railway had complained that excavations for water mains and gas lines on Water Street, Stanley Street, and Mines Road were not being properly filled on completion of the work. The Nelson Gas & Coke Works Company, still embittered by this skirmish with the street railway, now reminded the population that it had entered into its agreement with the city for the delivery of energy to residences and business firms on the understanding that its only competitor would be the city-owned electrical system. Obviously the supply of West Kootenay power posed a serious threat to the gas company.

The fight went on during the course of several more council meetings, finally resulting in a compromise. Council decided that the city would buy the surplus power specified in the tramway company's contract with West Kootenay, but that the city, not the tramway company, would distribute this power in Nelson. The advantages of this proposal for everyone except the gas company are obvious. Unfortunately, Mayor Houston maintained that such an agreement would eventually put the city's plant out of business. He decreed that the agreement would have to go before the electorate as a by-law. Council, perhaps overly optimistic about ratepayer support, decided to put the agreement to the voters on November 19, 1901.[37]

Extension of the Line

In the meantime, encouraged by backing from at least some members of council, the tramway company carried out improvements which it had been considering. In September 1900, the company applied for permission to move its tracks from Kootenay to Stanley Street, since the grade on Kootenay Street had proved to be far too severe. The change would see the new trackage leave Kootenay at Observatory, run along Observatory to Stanley, then up Stanley to the skating rink at Houston. Track already laid on a portion of Kootenay and along Houston would be taken up to provide the necessary rail. Permission was granted by council on October 1. Service was suspended beyond the carbarn

Car on Baker Street near Kootenay. The photo shows the line which ran to the CPR station.

during much of the construction period.

January 1, 1901 saw the opening of the new uphill line as well as the extension from Railway and Baker streets to the new CPR (formerly the Columbia & Kootenay Railway) station, which also opened that day. This new union station (built by the CPR and shared with the Nelson & Fort Sheppard Railway) was located two blocks south of the original Columbia & Kootenay station. January 1 also marked the closing of the old Nelson & Fort Sheppard Railway station in Bogustown.[38]

With the relocated line to the skating rink and the extension to the Canadian Pacific Railway station in place, a new service began on January 1, 1901. One car was to run from Stanley and Baker to the eastern end of the line at Lakeside Park, while the other ran from the new railway station up the hill to the skating rink. When traffic warranted, the third car would offer service from downtown to Lakeside Park, providing a ten minute service to that facility. For the new service to function, the passing track on Josephine Street was relocated to Front and Hall streets and put into service early in June. As Affleck comments, "It is ironic that the Front Street passing track, constructed to serve a western terminus at Baker and Stanley Streets, should have persisted for the remainder of the life of the street railway, while the Josephine Street passing track*, better . . .[located for] the belt line,**uphill service which eventually developed, should have disappeared."[39] This sentiment must have been echoed many times by others who tried to make a two-car schedule work during the subsequent history of the line.

On January 5, 1901, having improved its service to the skating rink, the street railway offered a five-cent fare to the rink's season-pass holders. For occasional skaters, the company offered combined streetcar transportation and skating rink admission for twenty-five cents on nights when the rink was open, an arrangement which came into effect in mid-February. In December, the company had arranged for a band to play at the rink on Tuesday and Friday evenings.***

The April 28th issue of the *NDN* announced that a reduction in service would take place on May 1. The article contains the first intimation that cars would no longer run through to the new Canadian Pacific Railway station. It notes that passengers who wished to be taken to the station were to notify the conductor. The cars would continue, however, to meet the 11:35 a.m. and 10:10 p.m. trains. A twenty-minute service would be offered with cars leaving the 'uptown (now Stanley and Baker streets) and the park end' termini on the hour and every twenty minutes. (It should be kept in mind that at this time the Josephine Street passing track was still in place.)

* This passing track was no longer required once the CPR station line opened on January 1, 1901. The rail and switches for the Front Street siding may have been taken from it. The Front Street siding was under construction on June 6 and in operation at least by June 10. [40]

** Actually a loop line. A true belt line is essentially a circle, and the cars on it do not travel to other parts of the system, but simply travel around the belt either clockwise or counterclockwise. Track on the uphill line in Nelson did not permit this type of operation, but merely turned the car around ready to return to the other end of the system.

***The rink concerts were still part of the picture in the winter of 1907-08. The skating rink, incidently, was built on the south end of Nelson because the ice froze more readily up there and did not thaw so quickly in the daytime. The difference in altitude between cemetery and lake level made for a marked difference in freezing level and snow fall.[41]

48

There was good news for regular streetcar patrons in the same issue. In an attempt to encourage its regular supporters, the company announced the reduction of its fare to five cents if ten tickets were purchased.

More Tragedy

During a violent storm on November 17, 1900, a tree fell across the W.K.L. & P. Company's power line from Bonnington Falls, cutting off the supply of electricity to the street railway and effectively putting it out of service until repairs could be made. The same storm drove the *Moyie* aground on the rocks at Midge Creek.

Slightly less serious was a runaway down the steep grade on Stanley Street which took place on December

CPR passenger train at the new union station about 1902. The station is still in existence although somewhat modified.

Paddlewheelers tied up at the Government Wharf at the foot of Hall Street

6, 1900. One of the two original cars, nicknamed *winter cars* because they could be used year-round, broke down at Stanley and Baker streets. It was moved to the track leading to the CPR station, and #3 was taken out of the barn to replace it. The first trip went well, but on the second trip down Stanley, the car's brakes failed shortly after it passed the carbarn. The crew consisted of Conductor William Campion who had been in the accident the year before and Motorman Coyle. Believing that he was about to see a repeat of the earlier tragedy, Campion jumped off, but Coyle stayed with the car and managed to bring it to a halt after it careened around the corner at Stanley and Baker.[42]

Cheated, the hill still managed to claim a victim, this

50

time the popular Donald J. Beaton, editor of the *Nelson Daily Miner*. About five p.m., Sunday, July 21, 1901, Beaton boarded a car at the top of Stanley Street. The rear vestibule on the winter cars was open, and he stood there to enjoy a smoke as the car made its way down the hill. When the car turned onto Observatory Street, Beaton lost his balance and fell out on the roadway, striking his head and shoulder. He was helped to the nearby home of John Horton, and a doctor was called. The latter examined the patient and felt satisfied that there was no serious problem. When he returned two hours later, however, he saw that Beaton had suffered a massive brain hemorrhage. Beaton died at about 8:30 p.m.[43]

Financial Difficulties

"The Nelson Electric Tramway Company was but one manifestation of the tremendous industrial development which took place in the Kootenay during the 1890s. Nelson had a meteoric rise and a long decline. The N.E.T. began operations as the decline set in, but both the City and the street railway refused to lie down and die."[44]

Much of the street railway's dilemna stemmed from the fact that in 1901 Nelson's population included only 5273 residents.*[45] Although it would be difficult for the tramway to generate profits in such a situation, Affleck believes that the street railway's financial problems were not the result of mismanagement. The firm's business plan " . . . reflected some sound thinking. The company controlled entertainment centres at both ends of the line, and held real estate for development along much of the line. Would that Nelson had developed a population of 20,000, much of it perched up in the heights of Fredericton. The fate of the early company might then have been much different."[46]

The seriousness of its financial position is indicated by a timetable change effective Sunday, September 29.

*Even in 1986, the city's population numbered only 8113.

The company proposed a single-car, forty-minute service before 11:00 a.m. and after 7:20 p.m. with a twenty-minute, two-car service in between. The first car would leave Bogustown at 7:00 a.m. The last car would leave Stanley Street at 10:20 p.m. and Bogustown at 10:40 p.m.

The by-law mentioned earlier, which was designed to help the tramway company dispose of its surplus electricity, was presented to the ratepayers on November 19, 1901. To the consternation of both the company and many members of city council, it failed by eight votes. What makes its defeat particularly difficult to understand is that the city was perennially short of power, and the proposed arrangement would have solved everyone's problems. The failure was especially serious for the tramway company. In anticipation of increased revenue from the sale of surplus power, the company had carried out various improvements during the fall of that year. On November 22, as a direct result of the by-law's failure, all employees of the street railway were given a week's notice of dismissal.[47]

Fortunately for the employees (and for the citizens who depended on the street railway), W.A. Macdonald, who was responsible for the tramway locally, received word that C.S. Drummond would arrive from England about December 18, and that nothing was to be done to close the line until he arrived in Nelson. The notice of dismissal was therefore cancelled. When Drummond learned that patronage was up 50 per cent over the previous year, he concluded that if the tramway could sell its surplus power to the city, many of its problems would be solved.

As a result of Drummond's visit, the mayor put a second by-law to the ratepayers, and, possibly as the result of a light turnout, it too failed to pass. On December 23, council, on its own initiative, agreed to buy power from the tramway company.

From the street railway's point of view, one good thing happened during this period - John Houston decided not to run for office in the 1901 civic election. He may have been unwilling to face the ratepayers after the collapse of the wooden power dam on Cottonwood Creek in August 1900. (Houston had attempted to solve Nelson's perennial shortage of water in the summer by raising the structure four feet.) In any case Houston decided to abandon local politics for the provincial arena, although he was re-elected as mayor in the 1905 municipal elections.

With funding somewhat more assured, the street railway agreed to carry out the minimum service called for in its operating agreement with the city. Maintenance was greatly reduced, and one of the two winter cars was sold to the British Columbia Electric Railway leaving Nelson on May 27, 1902 for the coast.[48] A second car was sold to the same system in 1905, but the only clue as to which one comes from a news item in *Railway and Shipping World* in 1905 which says, "The B.C. Electric Ry. has purchased the first car owned by the Nelson Electric Tramway Co. . . ."[49] "First car" would seem to indicate one of the closed cars, rather than #3. This report is interesting, since a newspaper statement of November 11, 1904 says that, "The larger cars are to be kept for holidays and special occasions." Service to the CPR station was also discontinued. *

The connection of the N&FS tracks with those of the C&K in 1897 later made it possible for CPR passenger trains to pick up passengers disembarking from the Crow's Nest Pass steamer right at the Government Wharf once this line opened in December, 1898. As a result, it was easy for passengers intending to take the train to ride the streetcar to Front and Hall streets from which it was just a short walk to the waiting train. A passenger would have the advantage of a better seat selection than would be the case if she or he boarded an already partially full train at the CPR station. * *

The entire system was shut down for repair from April 5 to June 4, 1904. When service resumed, the company announced that the schedule would be carried

* *Poor's Manual of Railroads* for 1903 states that as of June, 1902 the tramway company owned three miles of track of which only 2.65 miles were in operation, the difference being the length of the unused trackage to the CPR station.

* *Affleck suggests that the practice of boarding the train at the wharf continued until about 1930 when the railway line from Kootenay Landing to Nelson was completed, doing away with the steamers which previously provided this service.[50]

out by one car operating on a 40-minute headway.*

In the normal course of events, John Houston would probably have had much to say about the reduction of service mentioned earlier, but Houston had been elected as a member of the provincial legislature, and was away in Victoria. There were others, however, who believed that the tramway company's salvation lay not in cutting service, but in expanding it. For the most part the company's uphill route provided service to a part of the city where the company had real estate holdings. A possible extension which would serve an important residential development that was taking place as well as the new high school built in 1902 near the Latimer and Hendryx corner might leave Stanley Street at Latimer, work along Latimer to Carbonate, then along Carbonate to Park Street. To some extent service was provided to this area in 1910 when the uphill loop line was built.[51]

While the single car operation provided some relief to the beleaguered tramway, the outcome was almost inevitable. On October 11, 1904, council received a communication from the company proposing that since the street railway had lost money for five years, the city take over operation of the system. Council accepted, and a week later with both London directors of the company present, an agreement was concluded. The city would lease the line for four years beginning January 1, 1905 at a nominal rent of $5 per annum. Other terms in the by-law which council would subsequently put to the voters included the following:

a) The city was to lease the tramway's physical plant for four years, including a single-truck car which the company would obtain,** other existing rolling stock, roadbed, overhead lines, carbarn, substation, generating equipment and tools. The company's real estate holdings were not included.***

b) One-man operation was to be introduced after the 1905 elections on the understanding that, should the tramway company resume operation of the line at some future

*The term *headway* refers to the interval between one car and the next car travelling in the same direction on a route.

** The evidence suggests that the car acquired from the BCER in Vancouver was their #44, a single-truck car built by the Canadian General Electric Company in 1900. The car had a 21'6" body mounted on a truck built by Canadian Switch and Spring.[52] It arrived in Nelson "from the coast" on December 2, 1904. The *NDN* for the following day describes it as holding from 16 to 18 passengers.

***In 1921 the company still held real estate in the Nelson area. That year it sold five lots on Robson Street to the city for $1500 to make up the property required for the new Trafalgar School.[53]

*When Mason returned to England, he was put in charge of the South Metropolitan Tramways & Lighting Company at Croydon. He became engineer to the three London tramway companies and later played a major role in the development of the Feltham cars, an important class of English streetcars.[55]

British Columbia Electric Railway #40 built to the the same design as #44, the car sent to Nelson

date, it would also be able to operate with the one man system.

c) Should there be an operating loss, the company would assume 60% of such loss to a maximum of $1500 in any one year.

d) The tramway company was to lend its Manager, A.V. Mason,* to the city to provide assistance and advice during the changeover period. [54]

Ratepayers voted to pass the agreement in the form of a by-law on November 10, 1904.

Operating Problems

The city took over the line on January 1, 1905 with

Thomas Weekes as manager. City hall staff assumed the accounting functions, and the entire operation was the responsibility of council's street railway committee. The new system provided a forty-minute service, using the single-truck car recently acquired from the BCER, operating with a two-man crew.* Adherence to two-man operation may have reflected council's fears about accidents on the hill section of the system, especially during the icy conditions which prevailed during this period. The immediate reason was probably an unwillingness on the part of council to tackle the one-man car question. The question of one-man operation would be discussed many times in the years to come, but the system remained a two-man operation throughout its operating history.

The perils of one-man operation were illustrated on February 17, 1905 during the supper hour, when Conductor P. J. Clark was at the controls of the one-truck car while Motorman Leonard Gobey was eating his lunch in the rear vestibule. As the car swung down the Water (Front) Street hill east of the Cedar Street Crossing, it encountered on the track a horse-drawn sleigh bearing a load of slabs. The car crashed into the load of slabs, suffering considerable damage to its front. J. Rochon, driver of the sleigh, escaped without injury as did the sleigh itself, although his two horses were cut about the legs. Passengers H. Bird [a prominent citizen involved in real estate] and G.N. Gilchrist [the assistant postmaster], as well as Gobey, escaped without injury, but Mr. Bird's two young daughters suffered scalp wounds when they were thrown back in their seat. Acting motorman Clark suffered a leg injury which kept him off the job for an extended period.[56]

A second event, which took place April 6, 1905, was less serious but more spectacular. A flat car (probably a small four wheel handcar such as trackmen use) accidently became uncoupled at the substation and raced down Hall Mines Road and Stanley Street, finally derailing in front of the telephone company's office.

Despite these two incidents, the financial situation

*Two-man operation required both a motorman and a conductor. The motorman essentially operated the car, and the conductor looked after the passengers. Since some street railways about this time were beginning to encounter financial problems, they began seeking legislative permission to operate what were called 'one-man cars' in which one man carried out the duties of both motorman and conductor as a means of dealing with rising costs. This movement was bitterly opposed by the street railwaymen's unions for obvious reasons, and by the public who felt that a one-man car might not be as safe as one with a crew of two. Cars operated as one-man cars usually had to have special brake, power, and door systems, so that if anything happened to the motorman, the power would be shut off, the brakes applied, and the doors opened - all automatically.

improved to the point where early in June 1905, council announced that, while the forty-minute service would be continued, a twenty-minute service would be provided daily between 1:00 p.m. and 6:00 p.m. Cars were to run through once again to the original terminal at the end of the line on Houston, which would indicate that the routes had been cut back, ending probably at the carbarn. An even greater indication of prosperity was the decision to repaint the larger of the two cars. Unfortunately, that same week receipts fell off for the first time since the city took over. Consequently, at the end of June, council restored the forty-minute schedule except on Sundays from 1:00 p.m. to 6:00 p.m. when a twenty-minute service would be provided.

By 1908 the city was experiencing considerable difficulty in maintaining service. Only the small car could be operated owing to a shortage of repaired armatures. When snow came, the large car was not available to push the snowplow, and since the smaller of the two could not, service was irregular throughout most of January and February. At the end of January, thought was seriously given to closing down the system. One of the problems facing council was that its lease of the system was due to expire at the end of 1908, by which time all equipment had to be put into satisfactory condition for return to the original owners. The city fathers were reminded that the street railway was showing a loss on operations solely because of the money being spent on repairs, money which had to be spent whether the line operated or not. It was argued that, since the repairs had already been carried out, the line might as well operate. Council agreed, and by the end of February, maintenance and repair work had reached the point where both cars could be kept in operation.[57]

While the financial problems which were encountered during the four-year period might easily be blamed on successive councils, Affleck, himself an accountant, believes that the aldermen should not be criticized too harshly for the financial problems which arose during civic management of the line. He argues that:

> The profitable operation of a street railway involves the recovery of sufficient revenue to support the cost of periodic renewals and major renovations to rolling stock, roadbed, trolley wires and generating equipment. Railway accounting procedures at the time did not fully recognize the need to include in current operating costs a provision for the periodic costs of renewal and renovation, so that successive Nelson city councils should not be unduly criticized for a tendency to take into account wages and other routine operating costs, but to view renewal and renovation projects as unpleasant costly surprises from which the civic taxpayer should be sheltered. Such was the case with civic operation of a street railway line which was not in pristine condition at the beginning of the four-year lease, and which deteriorated steadily for lack of adequate upkeep.[58]

Disaster Strikes Again

Beginning Saturday, April 25, 1908, a succession of misfortunes took place affecting both the city and the street railway. Shortly before 11:00 a.m. as the big car was being moved out of the barn, its controller arced, blowing the circuit breaker. About half an hour later, at 11:20, the small transformer in the substation blew, igniting an oil switch and setting the structure ablaze. The fire destroyed the frame section of the building housing the electrical equipment of the street railway and the West Kootenay Power and Light Company. Firemen saved the newly-built brick portion belonging to the city.[59]

The following Monday (April 27) about 3:20 a.m., the carbarn itself burned to the ground along with the two cars inside.* The fire appeared to have begun in the workshed. Since there were no combustibles stored in the carbarn, and since no electrical malfunction was found, this second blaze was thought to be a clear case of arson.[60]

By superhuman efforts on the part of the city's electrical staff, power was restored to the city's electri-

*There is still some doubt as to which cars were destroyed. Les Hall was at the fire as a boy, and believed that one of the cars was #3, the open car. The other candidate was probably #44. The newspaper account already referred to says that two cars were burned. The information contained in Poor's Manual for the period ending June 30, 1908, shows only two cars in service which would support the newspaper article.

cal system by Monday night, but their efforts were in vain, since someone drained the oil from one of the transformers, once more plunging the city into darkness. Fortunately, the loss in both the carbarn and substation fires was covered under the city's agreement with the street railway.

Negotiations to Restore Service

Despite these setbacks, the desire for a street railway in Nelson was still very strong. Council met a month after the fire and wrote a letter to the street railway's parent company suggesting that, since revenues had begun to rise just before the fire, the company resume service with small cars so as to permit a more frequent headway. In return, the city would supply the street railway with free power from its new power plant on the Kootenay River, at least until revenues reached a certain level.

In response, the British parent company sent one of its London directors, E. Garcke, to Nelson, to take a look at the results of the fire, and to discuss the city's offer. Garcke informed council that his London office definitely did not wish to resume operation of the line, but was prepared to sell the line (excluding the tramway company's real estate holdings) *as is* to the city for $40,000 - an offer which the mayor and council promptly termed ridiculous. Eventually, in the spring of 1909, the ratepayers approved the purchase of the street railway's remaining assets, except for its real estate holdings, for $10,000, but in the meantime nothing further was done to restore service on the street railway system.[61]

E. L. Affleck, whose father, W. Lloyd Affleck was articled to Frank C. Green, the provincial land surveyor in Nelson at the time, includes an interesting anecdote about this period of inactivity. "In the spring of 1909 a newcomer to Nelson waiting patiently beside the street railway tracks at the west end of Baker Street hailed my father with the question, 'When may I expect the next street car to come along?' My father could not resist

making the following response, 'Well, I've been resid-ing here for the past three months and have yet to see anything moving on those tracks!'"[62]

Nelson in the late 1890s. The route of the Hall Mines aerial tramway is indi-cated by the arrow.

60

Chapter Four

THE NELSON STREET RAILWAY
COMPANY   1909-1913

Depression Strikes the Kootenays

BETWEEN 1898 AND 1903 the economic climate in the
Kootenays deteriorated substantially, although the local papers were careful not to draw this fact to the
attention of investors who had shown an interest in the
area. Factors contributing to the financial decline included: the gold rush in the Klondike which lured both
investors and prospectors from the area; the drop in
British investment as a result of the South African war;
the *eight hour* amendment to British Columbia's mining legislation which drove the smaller mines out of
business; the drop in the price of silver between 1900
and 1902; the attempts of the Guggenheim interests in
the United States to *discourage* competition from the
Kootenays in lead and zinc, and the collapse of mining
speculation in the Rossland area.

Transportation systems, closely tied to the mines'
welfare, naturally suffered along with them. The Great
Northern subsidiaries which operated steamboat and
railway service between Bonner's Ferry, Kuskanook,
Kaslo, Nelson, and Sandon lost thousands of dollars
each year. It was suggested on many occasions that the
Great Northern and the Canadian Pacific should com-
bine their competing services in the area, but neither

company wished to lose face and so continued their money-losing services in the Kootenays.[1]

Even though Nelson as a distributing centre fared somewhat better in all of this than its neighbour Kaslo, it did not escape unscathed. The general financial panic of 1907 caused severe problems for the Hall Mining and Smelting Company, forcing the smelter to shut down. After the failure of the smelter, most of the area's economic hopes were based on luring manufacturing plants to Nelson to take advantage of the cheap power available from the West Kootenay company's new Bonnington Falls power plant opened in 1908.

For a time, the Canada Zinc Company looked like a possible replacement for the smelter, as it attempted (without much success) to develop a process for separating zinc from galena in its plant on the edge of Bogustown. In the course of these experiments, the announcement was made by one of the company's scientists that platinum had been found in ore samples from the Granite-Poorman mine site. This triggered a short-lived mining rush resulting in the construction of many new homes on the northeastern slopes of the city. Unfortunately, when ore samples from the same area were examined by independent researchers, no platinum was found, and when a successful zinc smelter was constructed, it was at Trail, not at Nelson. By 1914, both platinum and zinc were dead issues, at least as far as the city's inhabitants were concerned.[2]

Nelson's citizens were still optimistic. There remained other potential contributions to Nelson's economic welfare. These included an abundance of Idaho White Pine suitable for clothespin manufacture, and the potential for a fine fruit growing industry, both of which contributed to the region's economy.[3]

A New Street Railway System

Despite the various financial setbacks which had occurred, these new ventures reinforced the continuing

Looking toward Nelson from the smelter site in the early 1900s

enthusiasm of Nelson's citizens for a street railway. On August 24, 1909 a group of local businessmen met to discuss the formation of the Nelson Street Railway Company. Formal organization of the new company followed on September 1, 1909 with incorporation taking place on September 7.[4]

Representatives of the new company approached council at its meeting of September 7 and requested the following:

1) free power for ten years;
2) a twenty-year franchise allowing the city the option to purchase at the end of that period;
3) guarantee of bond issues of $25,000 secured by the assets of the company;
4) tax exemption for ten years;

63

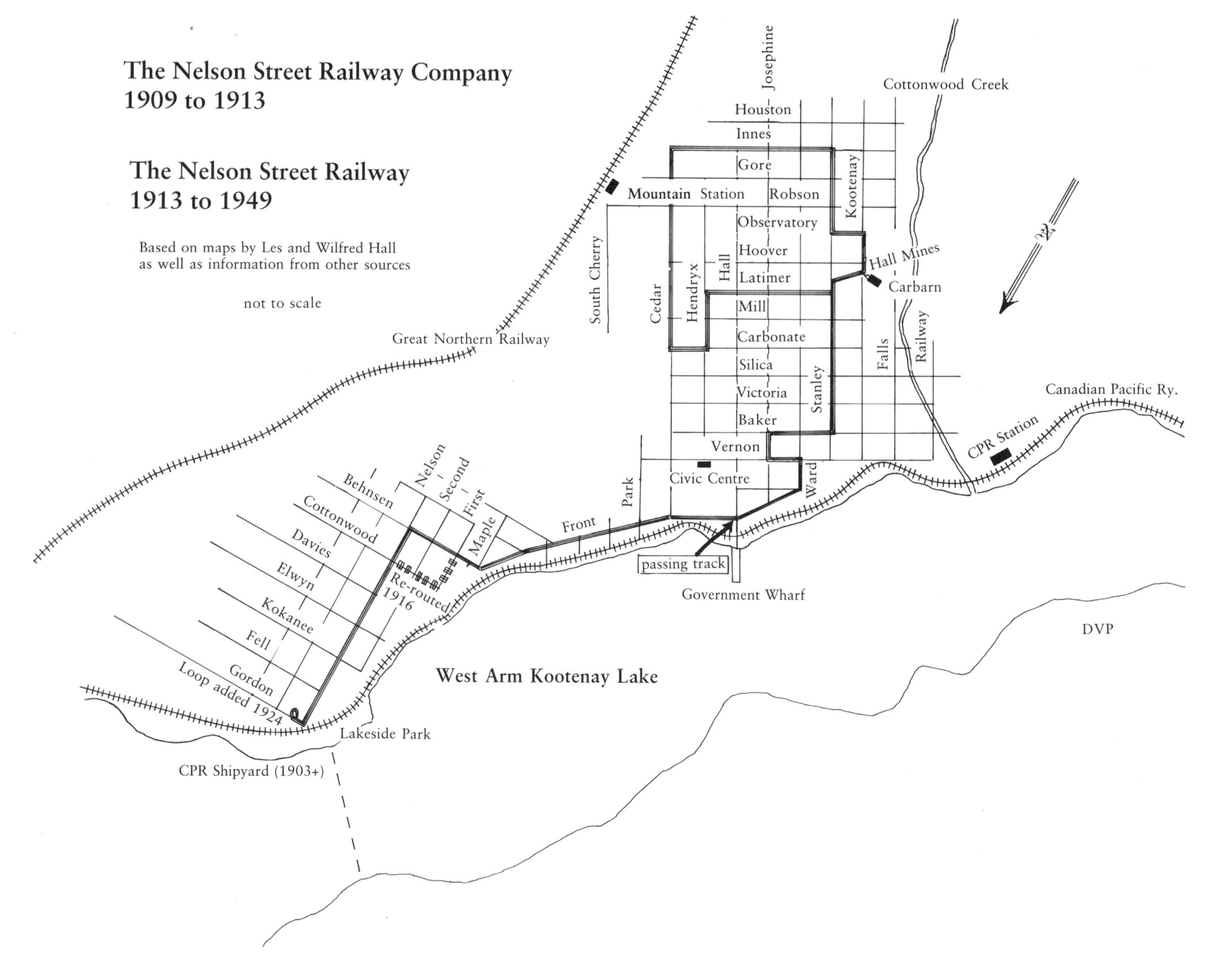

The Nelson Street Railway Company
1909 to 1913

The Nelson Street Railway
1913 to 1949

Based on maps by Les and Wilfred Hall
as well as information from other sources

not to scale

N
Josephine
Cottonwood Creek
Houston
Innes
Gore
Kootenay
Mountain Station
Robson
Observatory
Hoover
Hall Mines
Hall
Latimer
Carbarn
Cedar
Hendryx
Mill
Carbonate
Railway
Silica
Falls
Stanley
Victoria
Canadian Pacific Ry.
Baker
South Cherry
Vernon
CPR Station
Great Northern Railway
Civic Centre
Park
Ward
Behnsen
Nelson
Second
First
Cottonwood
Front
Davies
Maple
passing track
Elwyn
Re-routed 1916
Government Wharf
Kokanee
DVP
Fell
West Arm Kootenay Lake
Gordon
Loop added 1924
Lakeside Park
CPR Shipyard (1903+)

5) permission for the new company to build its carbarn on the site of the old burned-out NET carbarn at Hoover Street and Mines Road;*
6) permission to house its generator in a building to be constructed by the company on a site adjoining the present city sub-station at Victoria and Josephine streets (the newly-constructed building would then become city property);
7) lease of the existing street railway facilities to the company for ten years at a nominal sum. After this, the company would pay an annual rent not to exceed 6% on the capital of $10,000.[5]

Although the new company proposed to extend the existing street railway line four blocks across Gore Street to Hendryx Street, down Hendryx to Mill Street, up Mill to Park, down Park to Silica, down Silica to Ward, and down Ward to the present line on Baker, this was not the line that was finally built. Instead, at a meeting held on November 1, the directors determined that the new uphill section would leave Stanley Street and run "east up Latimer Street to Hendryx Street, north on Hendryx to Carbonate Street, east on Carbonate Street to Cedar Street, south up the Cedar Street hill to a summit at Innes Street, then west on Innes to join the existing line at Stanley Street."[6] The extension was designed to serve the new housing built in the area as a result of the *platinum rush* described earlier. Under the new plan, the usual route for a streetcar coming up Stanley Street would be to turn off Stanley Street at Latimer and follow the line just described.

A new and larger rink had been built on Hall Mines Road for the 1910 season, supplanting the Crystal Rink on Houston. The rail which had run to the old facility was lifted for use elsewhere.

The company intended to overhaul the present system, purchase a new motor-generator set, build a new carbarn and sub-station, and obtain a sweeper and two, double-truck cars with trailers.*[7] Given the existing grades on the route it is not clear just what had convinced the directors that a streetcar of that era could pull a trailer up the grades involved. Not surprisingly, the trailers were never purchased, and it would be a year before the sweeper arrived.

Council, who had begun to question whether it was legally authorized to operate a street railway, was probably more than pleased to find a private company willing to shoulder the burden and, on motion, supported their request unanimously. By-law #204, which not only covered the operating agreement between the company and the city, but also provided detailed rules of operation, was then submitted to the ratepayers. Council had made two changes to the company's original proposal, the first of which was that the fare was not to exceed five cents, even though the company had asked for a ten-cent fare. The five-cent fare doomed the new company from the beginning. The other change,

One of the new company's stock installment scrips made out to H.E. Dill

No. 135

Incorporated Under the Laws of the Province of British Columbia,
Companies Act, 1897, and Amending Acts.

Shares

Nelson Street Railway Company, Ltd.

Authorized Capital $50,000, in 51 Shares.   Head Office, Nelson, British Columbia.

Instalment Scrip

Received from *H. E. Dill*, of *Nelson B.C.*

the sum of *Six 25/100* Dollars, being the *1st* Instalment

of *25* per cent. on *25* Shares of the Capital Stock of Nelson Street Railway Company, Ltd., which said Shares are reserved and set apart for him or his assigns, on condition that he or they fulfil the terms of subscription and comply with the conditions of the Company's Charter and By-Laws.

Witness the Corporate Seal of the Company and the signatures of its proper officers in that behalf this *1st* day of *February* 19*10*

Secretary-Treasurer.   President.

perhaps more logical, was that in the event of a decision to sell within twenty years, the city should have first refusal. The by-law passed 259 to 10, and was ratified by council on October 11.[8]

Since the view had been expressed that the city could not legally enter into a contract with the operators of a street railway, to settle any doubt, the city requested that a bill be passed in the B.C. legislature granting it such powers. The bill, entitled *By-law #204, A By-law Respecting an Electric Street Railway in the city of Nelson, British Columbia*, was passed by the provincial legislature on March 10, 1910.

By-law 204 required the company to raise a minimum of $25,000. This did not prove to be an obstacle. The new street railway obviously enjoyed tremendous popular support, since the *NDN* for October 20 reported that sale of the company's stock had been amazingly large, and it was anticipated the last shares would be taken that very day. In fact, when the stock book was closed, $27,360 had been subscribed.[9]

On November 1,1909, when the board of directors of the new company held its first meeting, W.G. McMorris was elected president, G.W. McBride, vice-president, and E.B. McDermid, secretary-treasurer.[10] McMorris was a popular alderman, a principal in the *Nelson Daily News*, and the son of Nelson pioneer, Captain Daniel C. McMorris. McBride was a hardware store owner and an active Board of Trade member, while McDermid was a chartered accountant and a real estate and mining broker.[11]

On February 5,1910, an extraordinary general meeting of the street railway's shareholders authorized the issue of 5 per cent debentures to a total of $25,000. The company intended to spend $43,700 as follows:

a) a motor-generator set, 250-kilowatt capacity; from Allis-Chalmers-Bullock plus two sets of four, 40-horsepower motors - $11,000;

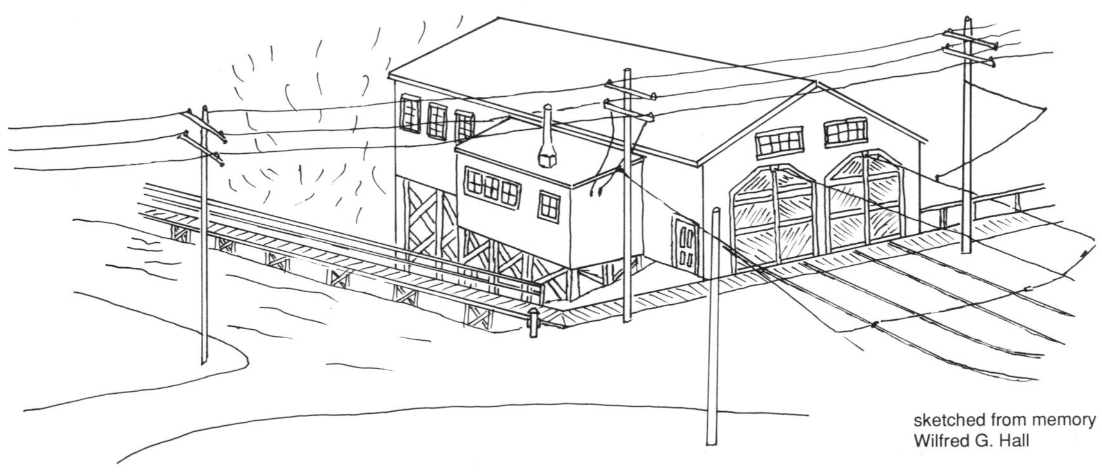

b) two, 44-seat, double-truck cars with trailers; Ottawa Car Company - $12,000 (the trailers were never delivered);

c) carbarns and machine shops - $2,500;

d) sweeper - $1,200;

e) extension of the line in the upper part of the city, about 8000 feet - $16,000, and

f) overhaul of the existing system - $1,000.

Tenders were also called for 123 tons of 56-pound rail, one left hand switch, and the necessary poles and ties.*

By April 7, the motor-generator had been installed, and the carbarn on Hall Mines Road had been completed. Construction of the roadbed and track was to be carried out under the direction of G.C. Mackey, the city engineer, and it was hoped to have the track completed within forty days. F.G. Poulton, who was appointed manager of the system as of May 1, 1910, was given the task of coordinating the restoration of the other parts of the system, as well as the new construction.[12]

The new carbarn measuring 25' by 80' was built on the northwest corner of Hall Mines Road and Hoover Street. Its roof and walls were constructed of corrugated iron painted dark red. Doors and trim were grey.

*The contract for the rail went to Evans, Coleman, and Evans who ordered it from the Illinois Steel Company in Chicago. The actual contract for the construction of the new section including roadbed, track, switches, poles, and overhead was let to L.G. Brandt of Nelson, with the poles being supplied by Jacob Knauf and Clarence Ogilvie.

By mid-June, the old track had been thoroughly overhauled and the overhead was being examined. Unfortunately, owing to a shortage of skilled craftsmen at the Ottawa Car Company and to problems with delivery of the trucks from the Brill plant in the United States, the two cars which had been ordered were delayed. By mid-July rails on the new extension had been laid and work had begun on the overhead wires.[13] By mid-September the street railway was complete except for the two cars.[14]

Finally the *NDN* reported on October 20 that the cars had been shipped. The article stated that they had been equipped with Westinghouse air brakes, which, regrettably, was not the case; they were fitted with hand brakes only. The same issue reported that William Rae, the inspector of railways for British Columbia (a former CPR machinist), had inspected the new extension, and that the overhead would be finished in the next few days. The company announced that it would soon be hiring motormen and conductors, married men being given preference.[15] It was hoped that with the arrival of the cars, a twenty-minute service would be provided between 6 a.m. and midnight.

Tickets, transfers, and timetable from the Nelson Street Railway

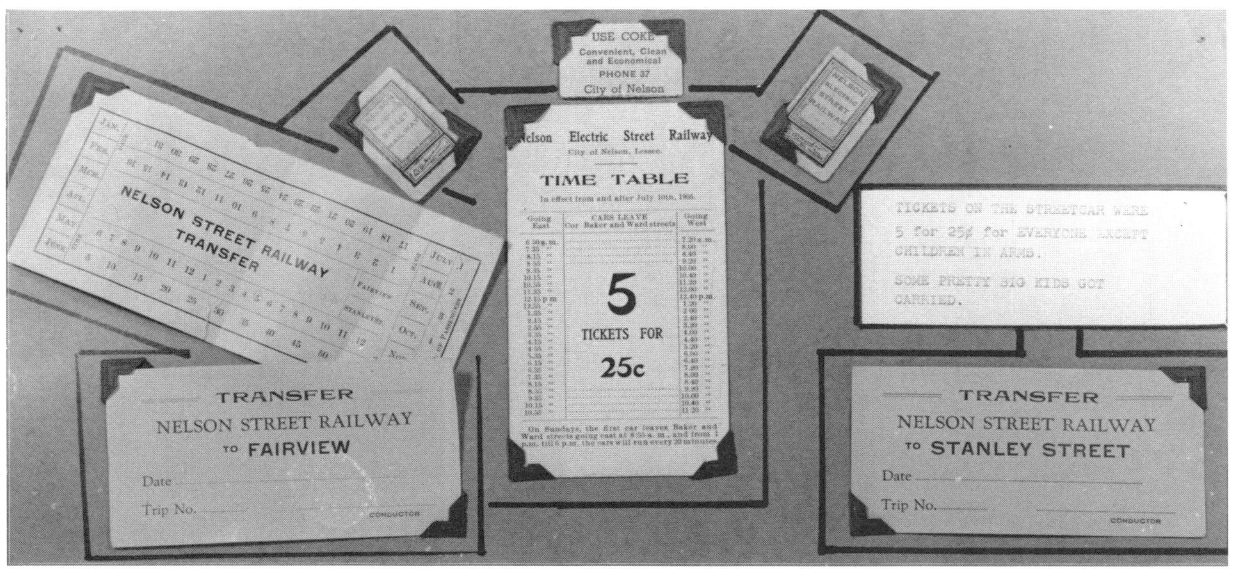

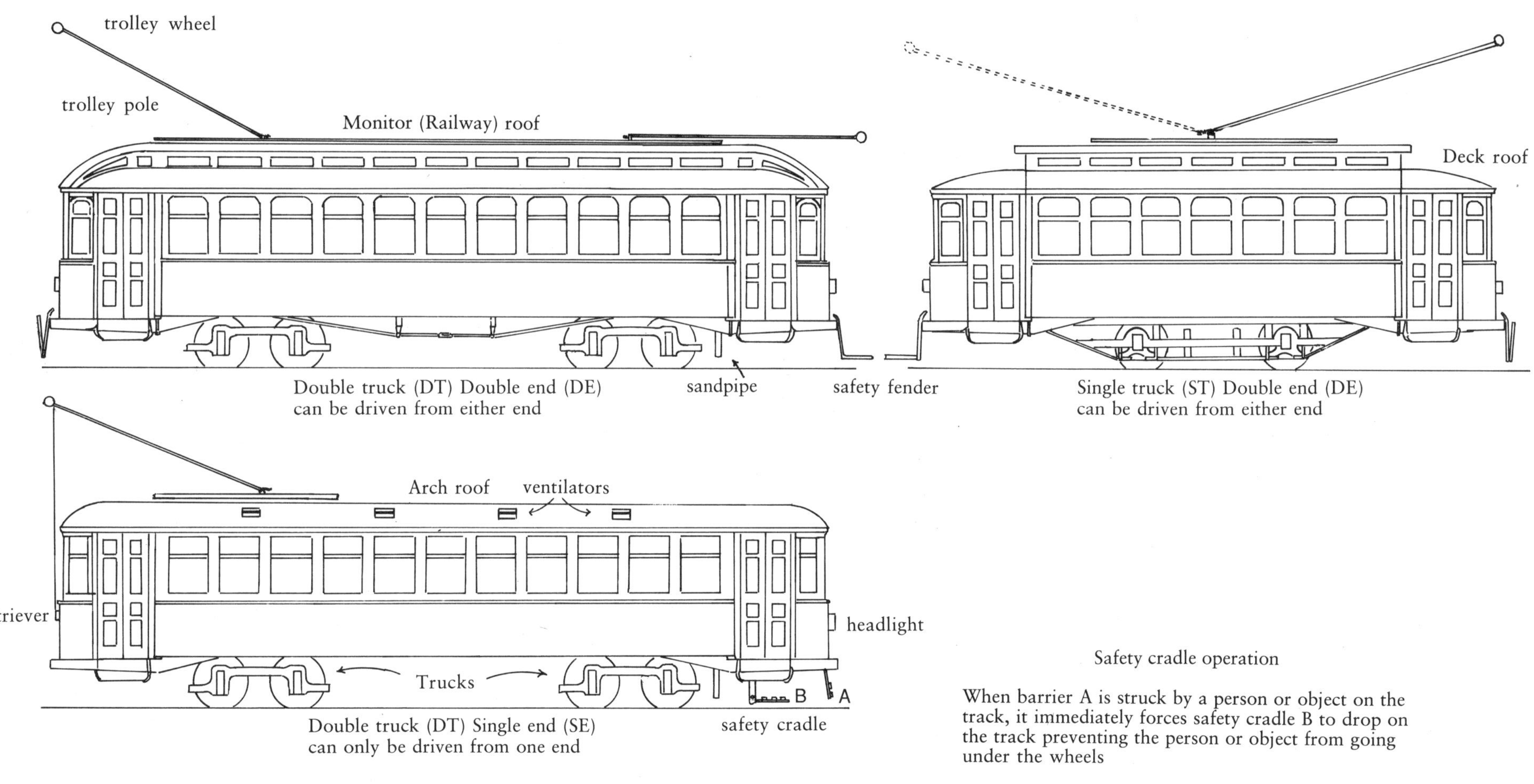

STREETCAR TERMINOLOGY

DVP

The board of directors stressed that no passes would be issued except to the superintendent and the police force. They were quoted in the *NDN* as saying, "We have decided to pay our fares in Nelson and we will expect the same of other citizens."[16] Adult tickets would be sold at six for twenty-five cents and children's at eight for twenty-five cents.[17]

The New Cars Arrive

Finally, on November 2, the citizens got to see their new cars which had arrived the night before. The *NDN* offered a description.[18]

... the eagerly awaited street cars reached the city last night. They were brought by barge from Kootenay Landing to Proctor and were rushed from the latter point to Nelson by rail. The directors of the street railway company hope to have them placed on the track at the foot of Hall Street and run up to the car barns on Hall Mines Road where they will receive the finishing touches preparatory to the first trial run. ... In spite of the unfavourable weather a number of citizens took an opportunity of obtaining an advance view of the new cars at the C.P.R. Station last night where they reposed for some time directly in front of the passenger platform ... In appearance the cars are all that could be desired. Olive green and cream in color and with fine grained wood work and brass fittings, the cars are both substantial and attractive in appearance. They are fitted with the most modern type of brakes [unfortunately these were still only hand brakes] and safety fenders ...

The street railway hoped to put the cars, numbered "1" and "2" like their predecessors, on its own rails and run them up to the carbarn for final checking. The original plan had been to put the cars on the tracks at the foot of Hall Street. When this proved to be impossible, they were unloaded instead near the CPR roundhouse and moved with a freight locomotive over temporary rail to the streetcar tracks at the west end of Baker Street. Unfortunately, the first attempt failed when the rails spread derailing a car, but it was still hoped to run them up to the barn that same afternoon under their own power.[19]

The same issue of the paper provided further details about the new rolling stock, reporting that the cars had electric heating and 30-inch diameter wheels instead of the more common 33-inch size. It was hoped that the combination of smaller wheels and a gear ratio of 69 to 15 would provide the necessary power to handle the system's rather steep grades. Unfortunately, the wheels supplied had a very narrow 2 1/8-inch tread, acceptable for cars running on pavement-embedded rails, but not for Nelson's open track. The cars also had a button at each seat by means of which the passenger could signal the conductor. The conductor then pulled a rope bell which signalled the motorman to stop. The ceilings were of bird's eye maple, and there were sliding vestibule doors which, when closed at night, made it easier for the motorman to see the track ahead of him. Unfortunately, there was no heat in the vestibule, and Wilfred Hall recalls that his father, George, had to wear heavy clothes and felt boots in order to keep warm. Conductors were expected to account for fares received through the use of

Cars 1 and 2 at the corner of Baker and Stanley streets. The steepness of the grade on Stanley Street can readily be seen in this photo. The car on Baker Street is on the line running to the CPR station.

Fare register

a fare register.

The trip up to Mines Road was not without incident. The first car derailed near the carbarn on Friday, November 4 and was put back on the track the next day. The second car was moved up Stanley only with great difficulty owing to the rails being covered with grease and rust through not having been used for so long. Sunday's *NDN* reported that the whole system would be checked by the inspector of railways, and it was hoped that the system would open about noon on Monday, November 7. Both cars would be moved to the corner of Baker and Ward streets where one would be started west by Mayor Harold Selous, the other east by Miss Grace Maurer, the youngest shareholder.

Streetcars Run Again

Unfortunately it was Tuesday before the formal opening took place, since Inspector Rae ordered some changes made before giving permission to begin operation. The track had been tested by #1 and was found to be in good shape except that the gauge needed correction at the corners of Baker and Stanley, and Ward and Vernon. The track gang also dealt with some soft spots in the roadbed which had developed at Cedar and Carbonate as well as at Stanley and Innis. Since Inspector Rae felt that the guard rails on the extension were too far away from the outer rail, they were bolted together and the spacing changed. The cars' brakes were found to need some adjustment, and the two sanding levers, one for each rail, were joined together so that their operation took only one hand instead of two as delivered. The rubber downspouts of the original sanders proved unsatisfactory and were replaced with flexible steel pipes.[20] Newspaper reports of November 11, 1910, imply that Inspector Rae had been extremely dissatisfied with what he found. As a result, Frank C. Ingram, a former employee of the old street railway, was appointed superintendent and assumed Poulton's duties.

A simple opening ceremony took place at noon on

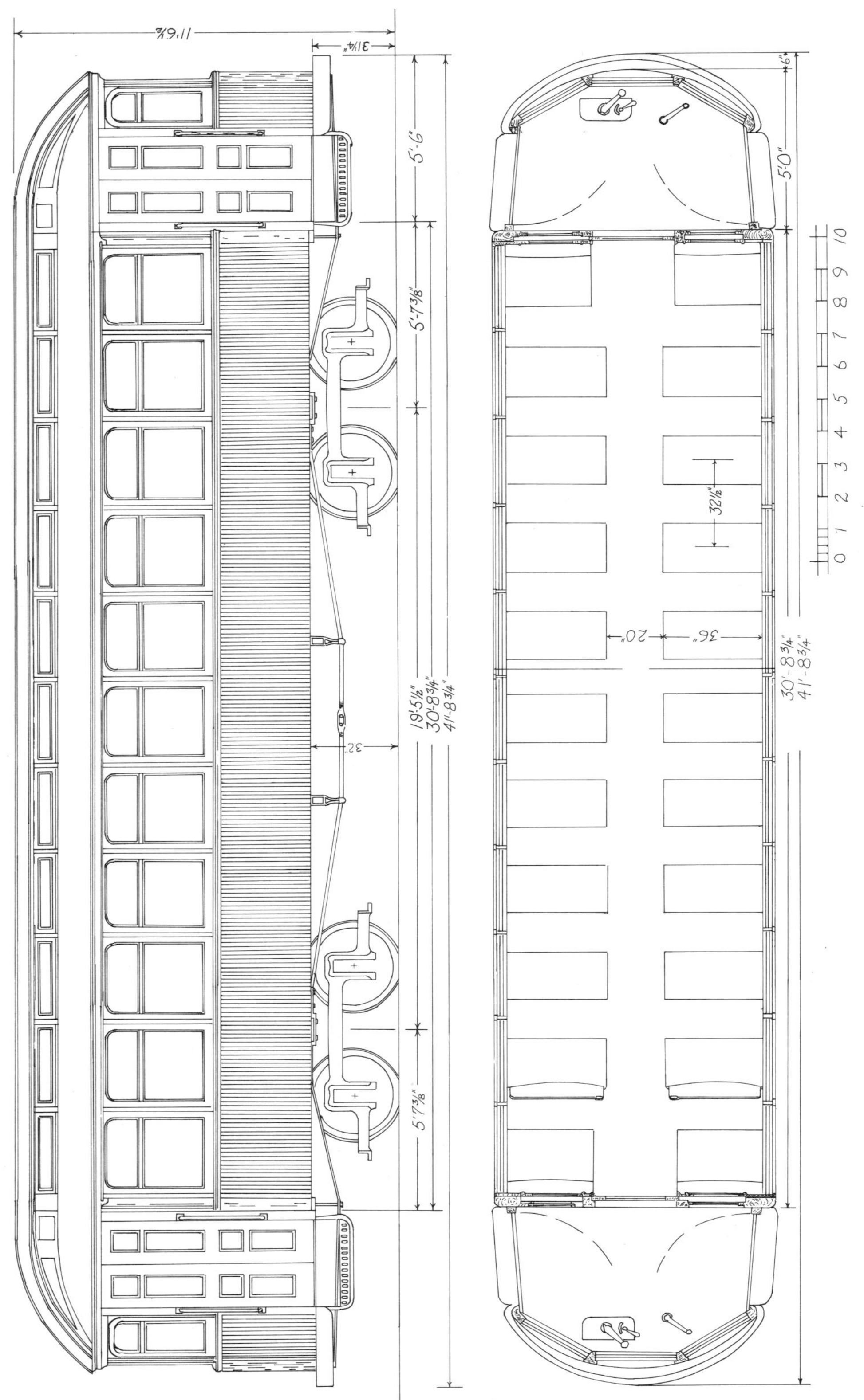

Tuesday, November 8. Mayor Selous started one car west, while Miss Grace Maurer started the other car in the opposite direction. Regular service began immediately, but was restricted to the old portion of the line. No service was to be provided on the extension until new wheels with a 3 1/2-inch tread arrived. Initially, only #2 was operated, since #1 had a bad flat spot on one of its wheels. (There had been concern that the flat spot might damage both the rail and the car. However, Inspector Rae stated that the flat spot would disappear as the car was operated.)

After some experimentation, it was found that the twenty-minute service which the street railway had announced at the opening ceremonies was not workable.* The schedule subsequently implemented showed that cars would leave Lakeside Park on the hour and the head of Innis Street on the half-hour, until the extension was open, or until both cars were back in operation. In the meantime, the superintendent tried out the new extension several times.

At first, business looked quite promising, since for the last week of November, fares had averaged slightly more than $40 per day. To raise additional revenue, the directors decided to rent advertising space on the cars.

The Nelson Street Railway's power came from the city's Bonnington power plant at 12,000 volts A.C. At the street railway annex to the municipal substation on Victoria Street, this was stepped down to 2300 volts A.C. to drive the street railway's motor-generator set which produced 500 volts D.C. The street railway's dependence on the city became a problem in late December when one of the city's generators failed. Repair time was estimated at about two months.

The remaining machinery could supply power for the city's lighting or for the street railway, but not both. Consequently, car service was cut back, to end at 4:30 p.m. daily. Unfortunately, power was supplied at a flat rate (i.e., no meters), providing little incentive for

*Based on later Department of Railways' correspondence, the inability to offer a twenty-minute service most likely had to do with the location of the passing siding on Front Street at Hall. The two halves of the line from this point were extremely imbalanced. The much longer segment included the hill section with all its inherent problems. It was unfortunate that in the reconstruction of the system, the original passing siding on Josephine between Vernon and Baker had not been relaid. This would have eliminated many problems over the years.

[facing page]
Cars 1 and 2 built by the Ottawa Car Company

householders to cut down on the use of electricity. In any case, the problem became academic, for in two days, as the result of a very serious accident, the entire street railway was closed down.

Another Runaway

About 11:30 a.m., December 21, 1910, #2, still with its narrow wheel tread, was climbing Cedar Street's 11 per cent grade, making the first trip on the new extension. The opening of the *belt line* was supposed to have taken place at an earlier date, but as mentioned, one of the city's generators failed, making it necessary to postpone the event. Two men had been sent out earlier to clear the rails of the mud and slush which had packed in the flangeways during the time the line was unused, but the car overtook them. In order to let the men finish past Latimer and Cedar, the motorman, L.G. Gobey, attempted to stop, but the car immediately began to slide backward down the hill. Brakes and sanders were applied without effect, so the brakes were released, and the power applied once more to allow the wheels to revolve and permit use of the brakes, unfortunately to no avail. The car left the track at the corner of Cedar and Carbonate, fell into a ten-foot gully, and landed on its side. Of its two passengers, Miss Blanche Hillman received cuts and a good shaking up, but a boy named William Wallach escaped virtually unharmed. Unfortunately, Superintendent Ingram suffered compound fractures of his leg, which later had to be amputated. Gobey, the motorman, had cuts, and G.W. Franklin, the conductor, was pinned beneath the car, but was only badly shaken up.

Following his investigation of the accident, Inspector Rae closed the line until air brakes and air-operated sanders were installed on the cars. He also ordered that before the line could be re-opened, three runaway switches had to be installed on the steepest part of Cedar Street.* The new 3 1/2-inch tread wheels would also add to the safety factor. Rae further suggested that the company purchase a third car as a replacement in case

* A runaway switch, sometimes called a safety switch, is constructed in such a way that a car coming down the hill out of control will automatically be diverted to a track usually buried in deep sand. The car stops when its wheels become embedded in the sand. Another approach is to have such a track run steeply uphill similar to highway runaway lanes for trucks.

of similar emergencies.[21] Regrettably, Inspector Rae was to return to Nelson on several similar occasions, occasions which for some reason always seemed to involve #2.

Meanwhile, #2 was carefully put back on the tracks and with a great deal of care moved back to the barn where it was found that, although the body and frame were not seriously damaged, one side was badly caved in. Repairs were estimated at $500.[22]

Since the steepness of the grade on Cedar Street undoubtedly played a major role in the incident, the city realigned the Cedar and Carbonate corner, and added enough fill on Cedar to reduce the grade to 8 per cent.

Westinghouse airbrakes and sanders were fitted to both cars; runaway switches were installed on Cedar, and the system re-opened to the public at noon, June 21, 1911, a full six months after the accident which

A Nelson Street Railway car in 1914, with motorman George Hall and conductor Jack Ingram, brother of Superintendent Frank Ingram

closed it. The new car crews included: L. Gobey, D. Chapman, and E. Manhart, motormen, and G. W. Franklin, H.D. Arnold, and D. Phillips, conductors. Superintendent Ingram was fitted with an artificial leg, and came back to supervise the line.* The accident and the resultant modifications to the cars produced such a drain on the company's finances that a drive for subscriptions for a further $10,000 had to be launched.[23]

While no schedule was available for the first few days, it was announced at the end of June that one car would leave the barns for the shipyards on Front Street (the site of the present R.C.M.P. headquarters in Fairview) at 6:30 a.m to permit the men who worked there to reach the Lakeside Park terminus by 7:00 a.m. The car would then provide fifty-minute to sixty-minute service until about 9:40 a.m. when crew and passengers would change to the other car at the carbarn and allow the first car to be taken in for maintenance, after which it would be returned to service about 11:30 a.m. This

*Wilfred Hall recalls that as a young lad at work in the carbarn he would "get very busy" when Superintendent Ingram's approach was signalled by the *thump* of his wooden leg.

The sweeper after rebuilding in 1921

schedule provided a thirty-minute headway, since the second car would run until 8:30 or 9:00 p.m. The service ended at 11:15 each night. Essentially this was the schedule which was followed to the end of streetcar operation, with the addition some years later of one more trip at night.

Arrival of the Sweeper

On December 8, 1911, a snow sweeper manufactured by the Ottawa Car Company, made its debut during a snowfall and was declared an unqualified success. This equipment had been included in the original estimates, but was not purchased immediately. Snow was often heavy in Nelson, and before the sweeper's arrival, the cars had been fitted with spring steel scrapers in an attempt to keep the tracks clear. There were even times when it was necessary to run the cars all night to keep the line open.

Financial Problems Return

The new company might have been financially successful except for several factors. The most serious problem was the city's small population. Even today the population of Nelson is not large, and in the early 1900s it was fewer than 6000 residents.[24] Despite the city's numerous hills, a determined person could walk downtown in ten to fifteen minutes, and if the cars appeared to be late, many chose to do just that. The five-cent fare and the requirement that the cars have two-man crews resulted in high operating costs and low income. The collapse of the short-lived platinum boom meant that revenues expected from the new loop line up the side of the mountain did not materialize. Finally, the accident, and the delay in re-opening the line, with its attendant expenses and loss of revenue, was a set-back from which the company never fully recovered.

An early postcard showing a car
on Baker Street

Chapter Five

THE NELSON STREET RAILWAY 1913-1949

The City Takes Over

WITH THE SUPPORT of a sympathetic city council, the tramway company managed to weather its financial problems of 1912. During 1913, its financial situation was so precarious there were almost continual suggestions in the local paper that the city purchase the system. Finally, to ensure continued operation, the city agreed, and for a second time the ratepayers were obliged to buy out a private company.

A by-law passed on December 29, 1913 empowered the city to take over the street railway, to spend $30,000 to cover debts and improve facilities, and to issue $16,000 in twenty-year bonds bearing interest at five per cent. The bonds were issued to the company's shareholders at the rate of 50 per cent of the value of shares held in the old company. Official transfer to the civic-owned Nelson Street Railway took place on February 1, 1914. Council appointed a committee to look after street railway matters, but responsibility for day to day operation remained with Superintendent Ingram.

The first major improvements carried out included further regrading of Cedar Street from Carbonate to Innes Street in 1916. Two bad curves at First and Behnsen and First and Cottonwood in Fairview were eliminated by relocating the line to run east on Behnsen Street to its intersection with Nelson Avenue. The 45-pound rail on the hill up Front Street was upgraded to 60-pound. Overhead wire was brought up to a standard height of 22 1/2 feet and replaced where necessary. Both cars were stripped, and thoroughly overhauled.[1] Once again, the future looked bright.

Another improvement frequently discussed but never implemented was the relocation of the passing track on Front Street at Hall. As mentioned in a previous chapter, the passing track was installed at this location when two routes were operated - one running from the downtown area to Lakeside Park, the other from the downtown area up Stanley Street to Innes. For the route running from the park to downtown, the Front and Hall Street location made good sense. Once the two routes were combined, it no longer did, because the location was only one-third of the way from the park to the end of the line at Innes and Stanley Streets. It was therefore

Cars 21 and 22 (formerly 1 and 2) pass at Hall and Front streets.

suggested that this siding be taken up and relocated on Josephine Street between Vernon and Baker, (roughly halfway between the two termini) where such a siding once existed. This relocation would have enabled the city to offer a twenty-minute service instead of the existing thirty-minute one. It would also have allowed a more frequent service when the city purchased a third car in 1924.

Regrettably, no action was ever taken, possibly because the location of the passing siding had also been dictated by its proximity to the City Wharf, a scant block away on the waterfront. Two cars would meet at the siding, each headed in a different direction, and pick up passengers from the evening *crow boat* (the paddlewheeler which until 1930 connected with the CPR's Crow's Nest railway line at Kootenay Landing) or an excursion steamer. The sixty minutes which each car was given for a round trip fitted in well with the Front and Hall streets location. A change to a forty-minute service would have required relocation of the passing siding to Josephine and Vernon streets.

Such a move (or even the addition of a second siding) would have solved an operating problem that was to bedevil the system for the rest of its life. The short section of relatively level track from the passing siding to Lakeside Park paired with the much longer and more difficult uphill section required the park-bound car to lay over for ten minutes when it reached the park in order to meet its colleague at the passing track on the return trip. Movement of the siding would have permitted better service to the Fair Buildings on Vernon Street (site of the present Nelson Civic Centre) while allowing for twenty-minute service. Unfortunately, the project would have required additional funds, and at the time further borrowing was out of the question.

During the first few years after the city took over the system, there were no major accidents. This happy situation changed on the afternoon of October 12, 1916, when three-year-old David (Dai) McLeod was waiting with his mother to catch the eastbound car at Ward and Baker streets. Just as the car with George Hall at the controls passed the pair, the little boy, who had been playing with a ball, dropped it. Before anyone could stop him, he ran under the car to retrieve it. His left foot and leg were crushed beneath the rear wheels of the car.* When George Hall got home at the end of his shift, he could neither eat nor sleep. "The memory of the child's screams was to haunt the kindly George Hall for the remainder of his life."[2]

In yet another incident, when motorman Freed came down Stanley Street to the corner of Observatory late one night, he thought he saw a man waiting to board the car. Since passengers always got on and off via the rear doors, he turned the corner and was about to stop the car with the rear doors beside the man when the latter suddenly fell in front of the car. He put the car's brakes into emergency, but it was too late. Freed felt a bump as the man's legs were severed below the hips. The motorman and his conductor jumped to the ground in a state of shock and looked under the car. Seeing the man's body under the car, they grabbed his coat sleeve and pulled him out. There were no signs of life - but neither was there any blood. They had been taken in by a dummy! The night in question was October 31, 1917, and Freed and his conductor were the victims of yet another Halloween prank. Sergeant Stewart of the city police tried to identify the clothing but with no success.[4]

Halloween was always a trying night for car crews especially along Cedar Street where it became a tradition to place outhouses on the streetcar tracks. Prior to the construction of the native-stone shelter at the Lakeside Park loop in the 1930s, the frame shelter which preceded it was regularly uprooted that evening. As in every city with streetcars, it was also a night for having trolley poles pulled off the wire.

Another Look at One-Man Operation

By the end of the First World War, it was apparent that

Motorman George Hall with his conductor, Harold Bellis, circa. 1914

*Three decades later, in 1946, a little girl ran out in front of a car driven by Austin Moore. When the crew stopped the car, they found her between the trucks. She was taken to hospital and found to have suffered only scratches.[3]

*Fare collection in a pay-as-you-enter (PAYE) car was quite different from the procedure followed earlier. On the early streetcars, the passenger would board the car and find a seat. The conductor moved through the car collecting fares in a hand-held farebox, known to car crews as the *coffee pot*. After collecting each fare, he pulled a rope to record the payment on a fare register mounted on the end wall of the car. In Nelson, when the conductor turned in his coffee pot to the office at city hall, then located at Ward and Vernon streets, the amount of money in the box had to talley with the amount shown on the fare register. When cars were crowded, it was usually impossible to collect all fares.
[Continued on the following page]

the system would continue to lose money. Any hope of using revenue to finance renovations and expansion was now gone. In fact, by early 1919, council was seriously considering ways of cutting costs. Consequently, when Inspector Rae was asked about the possible use of the pay-as-you-enter (PAYE) system* in Nelson as a money saving measure, he replied:

I am of the opinion . . . that what is wanted there is the *One-Man Car . . .*** In order for the Nelson St. Ry. Co. to adopt the One-Man system they would certainly have to go to some expense in alterations with regard to re-arrangement of their vestibules and several parts of equipment for the operation of safety devices which are applied to a car of this type. However the outlay would easily be repaid to the Company from the wages saved on the elimination of the second man on the car.[5]

George Hall standing beside his car at the Fairview terminus about 1914. Mrs. Notman (standing in the doorway) and an unnamed passenger watch the photographer with interest.

Rae took advantage of a visit to Nelson in the summer of 1919 to discuss the one-man car question with city officials. On his return to Victoria, he informed the chief engineer of the Department of Railways that he had raised the matter with Mayor McDonald and Superintendent Ingram, discussing with them the railway's characteristics, Nelson's climatic conditions, and the cost of converting their present cars to one-man operation. He reported that Mayor McDonald was of the opinion little could be gained in making this change.[6]

The discussions about one-man car operation would continue sporadically for some fifteen years, but no change was ever made, largely because of the expense involved in converting the cars and in installing the required safety devices. There was also the consideration that Nelson was a small community, and the car crews were popular with the inhabitants. Layoffs would have been unpopular with the line's passengers, who probably also felt safer with a two-man crew given the city's hilly nature.

The crews had endeared themselves to Nelson's residents over the years by the personalized service they offered. If a patron was known to have difficulty walking, as long as he or she was in sight, the car waited. In general the crews stopped for passengers wherever they were. Baby carriages and even groceries were carried on the safety fender.[7] Of course, the buggy asked for later would invariably be at the bottom of the pile! While there were restrictions on the number of passengers carried, D.S. Webster, one of the motormen, recalls that one New Year's Day, when a hockey game with Trail was being played at the arena, the load reached 113 passengers. The car was so tightly packed that passengers had to pull the communication cord for the conductor, since the latter was unable to reach it.[8]

Sweeper *Done In* by Barn Mate

In June 1921 another accident occurred which might have had tragic consequences had circumstances been

[Continued from the previous page] With the PAYE system, the conductor stayed in one place (usually at the door where the passengers boarded) and the passenger would drop the fare in a permanently mounted farebox. All fares were collected, which created some opposition to the PAYE system among those citizens who had mastered the art of avoiding the conductor under the old system. Unfortunately the time it took to load a car during rush hour also increased as a result of the need to buy tickets or obtain change from the conductor.

**A one-man car is built so that passengers enter and pay at the front door thus reducing the need for a conductor at the rear of the car. In addition, in order to ensure safety, the car is usually equipped with what is often called a *dead-man* control. Should something happen to the motorman, power is shut off automatically, the brakes are simultaneously applied, and the car's doors open.

* Inside a streetcar controller is a set of copper segments mounted on a central shaft. When the controller handle is rotated, the shaft turns, and the segments make contact with a set of fixed contacts or *fingers*, thereby determining, by adding or cutting out some of the electrical resistance, just how fast the car will go. As with any electrical contact, the surfaces of these fingers must be kept clean. In addition, during normal operation a very fine copper dust will form inside the controller as a result of the friction of the two surfaces. This dust must be removed, since if it is not, it can ignite, creating the risk of fire.

slightly different. The infamous car #2 made a determined effort to *do in* its barn mate, the sweeper. The story of this unusual accident was recounted by Wilfred Hall, son of Superintendent George Hall, in his talk to the Nelson Old Timers given on March 16, 1981.

The sweeper had been stored for the summer against the rear wall of the barn at the end of one of the two tracks. One of the maintenance men was responsible for cleaning the inside of the car's controllers,* and was accustomed to carrying out this task sitting on a very short stool so that he could more easily see inside the controller. Unfortunately, while working on #2 (which shared the track with the sweeper) he failed to notice that the pole was still on the wire and the car's circuit breaker (which also acts as an on-off switch for the car) was still closed allowing current to reach the controller. When he moved the handle of what he thought was a dead controller to get at the next set of fingers, the car began to move forward, pushing the sweeper out

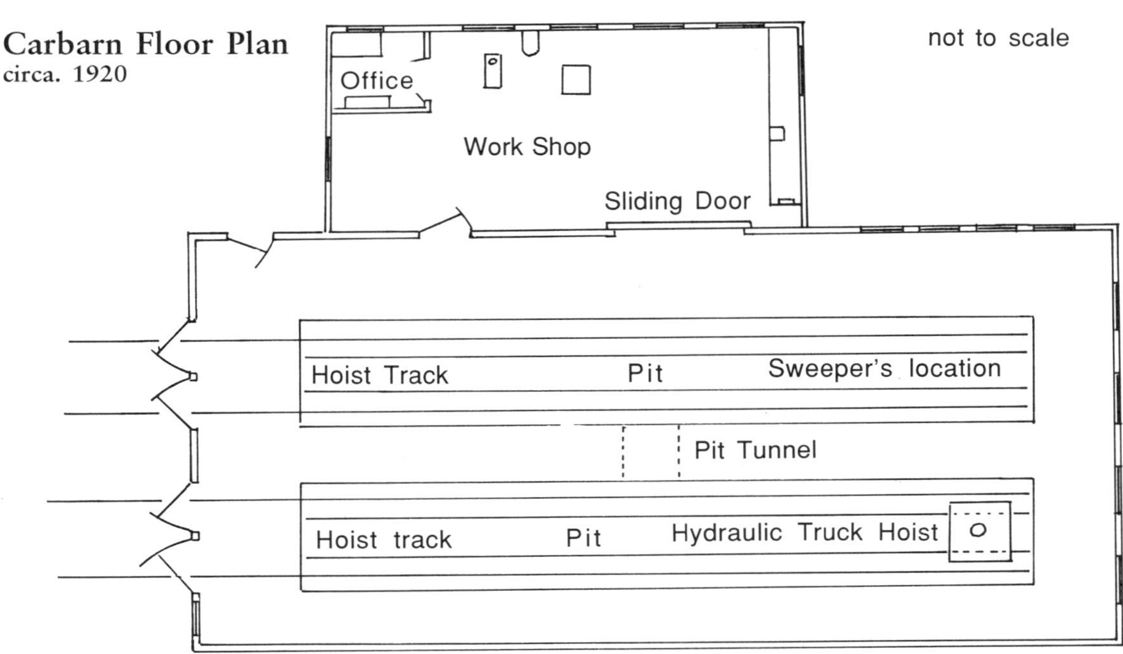

Original drawing by Wilfred Hall

through the end of the barn into a ravine (a drop of about thirty-five feet) where it came to rest upside down. The maintenance man's only intimation that something was wrong came when he felt the car he was on begin to move. Fortunately the streetcar stopped part way out of the barn when its front wheels ran out of rail jamming the truck against the floor of the structure. As Hall concludes, "The car was pulled back into the barn, the wall repaired, and the sweeper truck hauled up and [the sweeper] rebuilt." The city obtained a set of plans from the BCER, who had designed and built most of their own sweepers, and constructed a new body following BCER design. Repairs cost $800.

Attempts To Improve Service

In 1921, Alderman Shaw, chairman of council's street railway committee, staunchly supported by Alderman L.H. Choquette, tried to implement a twenty-minute service during the middle part of the day in an attempt to increase patronage on the system. Since Inspector Rae was once more in Nelson on May 21, he checked the actual operation of the cars, and concluded that a thirty-minute service was much more realistic. His

View from inside the carbarn showing the hole in the end wall

The sweeper upside down in the ravine while #2 surveys the scene from above

comments, made in a letter to Mayor Charles McHardy, offer some insight into the operating problems faced by the tiny system.

With reference to my interview with you and Committee on the 21st inst., I am herewith attaching check of the cars made on this date; . . . the time was so varied that it was almost impossible with the present location of your switches to maintain the twenty minute service as advertised. As there is practically from three to six minutes lost on every trip at the switches and no time being allowed at the terminals, it seems to me that it will be impossible to maintain this schedule. There is a possibility however of some changes being made to your line in the Fairview District and the placing of a switch on Josephine Street between Baker and Vernon. This would make a better meeting point for the cars.

At the time of making this check very close attention was given to the way the Motorman and Conductor handled their car and I felt satisfied that they were making every endeavour to maintain the schedule . . .

The general practice in making out schedules is to see that the car has ample time to arrive at their meeting points on time and in order to do this, a few minutes lapse time has to be allowed at terminals.

Another feature I observed was that you are not making the proper connections with the Ferry at Lakeside. [This was the Government Ferry which ran every hour between Nelson and the north shore of the West Arm. The present Highway 3 bridge crosses the Arm at the same location.] This must cause an inconvenience both to the Ferry and the Street Railway.*

I was also informed that one of the machines for taking care of the power for the line was under repairs, and the machine now in operation does not take care of the service, especially when the two cars are ascending grades at the same time. This was very noticeable and greatly decreases the speed of cars ascending grades and owing to the location of your line it would be a very dangerous practice to allow Motormen to make up speed on descending the grades.**

In order for the City to operate this line it is absolutely

* Affleck believes that whatever problem existed about making connections in the 1920s had been resolved by the 1930s when, ". . . the ferry made a point of waiting for street car passengers and vice-versa. Ferryman George Clerhiew set a very good example in this regard."9

**Old-time Nelson residents recall that some motormen did release the brakes allowing the car to run free downhill on Stanley Street!

The end of the carbarn showing the hole made by the sweeper

necessary that another car be procured; although at the present time your cars are in very fair condition, it is impossible to keep them in proper repair and maintain your schedule daily, when you have not another car that you can place on the run when extensive repairs are required.

I noticed in several places that the trolley wire is getting very thin and requires replacing, also on Innes Street the grass is allowed to grow to considerable length on the tracks and I consider [it is] becoming dangerous owing to the grade on this street especially on a wet day when the grass would get on the rails it would make it exceedingly slippery. I might say I called these matters to Mr. MacGuire's attention and he informed me this would be taken care of at once . . .[10]

As just mentioned, Chief Inspector Rae, along with Mr. MacGuire, the city engineer, checked the timing of the two cars and found a wide variation in the operation which only served to underline the need for a half-hour schedule. In a letter sent the same day to Chief Engineer Proctor of the Department of Railways, Rae reiterated his suggestion that the service be a half-hour one, since he felt that this would be the best the line could do. The thirty-minute service would also improve connections with the government ferry which ran every twenty minutes during daylight hours, hourly after dark.

As Rae suggested, the street railway's problems would not be easily solved:

This is a matter which has to be handled very delicately as this Railway is under Municipal ownership and the citizens are very much divided on the operation of this railway as it showed every year operating at a loss, and I fail to see where it could be improved on very much as there is not enough population to warrant a street car system. You will note that this check [referred to above] was made on a Saturday and will give you a fair idea of the number of passengers that are carried . . . [an average of sixteen per trip].

They are taking up the question of the one-man car and you will note that I informed the Committee that as this matter was now being taken up with the Department I was not in a position to make any definite reply. However I am of the opinion that a one man car could be operated there if a car of the double truck type was used. This I consider necessary owing to the excessive grades that this line is operating on as you would require practically a double truck car for braking power.[11]

The experiment of providing a twenty-minute service had to be abandoned in July of that year, even though the new approach did attract more riders. Since the schedule problem could be solved by relocating the passing siding, Aldermen Shaw and Choquette continued their efforts to obtain the $250 this would cost. Unfortunately, some of their colleagues were of the opinion that improved service would only wear out the equipment sooner, and, perhaps worse, make the purchase of a third car necessary.

Those who supported the street railway invited H. M. Lloyd, a B. C. Electric Railway mechanical engineer from Vancouver, to assess the situation. Lloyd felt that while the car bodies themselves were in excellent condition, the Allis Chalmers motors which powered the cars were now very much out of date. He recommended that:

a) two single-truck, one-man Birney* cars be purchased for regular use on the line;

b) the existing two cars be renovated and converted to one-man operation;

c) a 20-minute service, using three cars, be offered for a limited period during the day;

d) the carbarn be relocated to a site near the railway and the Nelson Iron Works.[12]

A Third Car Purchased

If some council members were unwilling to spend $250 for a passing siding, their reaction to Lloyd's report may easily be imagined. Meanwhile the breakdowns which council feared were not long in coming. Indeed, interruptions to service for this reason were a common theme throughout 1922. By 1923, Alderman Shaw was no longer involved in street railway matters, but probably to the great relief of those responsible for the street railway, Alderman Choquette had become mayor. As such, he was able to bring his influence to bear on provision of funds for maintenance of the system. During this time, Inspector Rae again recommended the purchase of a third car to allow proper maintenance to be carried out on the other two, combining this suggestion with a gentle reminder that he had the authority to revoke the line's operating certificate. He also recommended that the existing cars be converted to one-man operation. While council was still very much opposed to this, its members reluctantly concluded that a third car was necessary.

Consequently, on July 15, 1924, council voted to purchase a second-hand car from the Preston Car & Coach Company for $3000.* Preston's manager, Don Campbell, often acted as an intermediary in the purchase of second-hand equipment for Canadian street railways. His unique contribution to small systems was that he could often persuade the supplying street railway to carry out necessary repairs and alterations before shipping the second-hand car to its new owners. Most of the supplying systems were large operations for which this was a minor problem, while such renovations would have been difficult for the smaller purchasers. Campbell's approach was undoubtedly greatly appreciated by many small Canadian systems.

The new car was purchased from the Cleveland Railway Company. Built in 1906 by the Stephenson Car Company as the Forest City Railway's #3334, on absorption of that line by Cleveland, it was rebuilt in 1908 as a single-ended car and re-numbered as #934. It remained in service in Cleveland until 1924 when it was retired and sold to Nelson as Nelson's #3.

Number 3 was single-ended, so the existing cars were

*The Preston Car & Coach Company, located in Preston, Ontario, was one of Canada's major builders of street railway rolling stock, another being the Ottawa Car Company. Don Campbell, its first manager, had many contacts in the United States, especially in Cleveland, Ohio, where he had worked for the Kuhlman Car Company, builders of many of Cleveland's streetcars. He was in a unique position to obtain second hand street railway equipment from the Cleveland system for Canada's smaller street railways. The Preston Company was taken over by the J.G. Brill Company of Philadelphia in 1921.

*A single-end car can only be operated from one end and requires a turning loop at each end of the line, while a double-end car can be driven from either end, and does not require a loop. At the end of the line, the crew of a double-end car pulled down the trolley pole at the rear of the car, and put up the pole at the other end of the car. The motorman would carry the brake and controller handles to the controls at the opposite end of the car. His conductor would walk the length of the car and flip over the reversible seat backs so that passengers would still be facing the front of the car when it retraced its route.

Car #3 (as later renumbered 23) at Lakeside Park

also modified for single end operation, and a turning loop built at Lakeside Park.* The hill portion of the system already formed a loop, so no alterations were needed at that end. However, the carbarn was expanded to house all three cars and the sweeper.[13]

The new acquisition arrived on December 22, 1924, and until it cleared customs was parked on a siding near the City Wharf. One very noticeable difference was its red and cream colour scheme. The shiny paint undoubtedly covered a multitude of scars from #3's many years of service in Cleveland. The other cars were subsequently repainted to match, and the new colour scheme continued to the end of the system's operation. Only the sweeper retained the original moss green livery.

On December 27, 1924, #3 was moved to the street railway's tracks and put into service on Tuesday, December 30, an event which the *NDN* duly reported.

Nelson's new street car #3 was put into commission on a regular run yesterday afternoon. Previous to taking over the run from car #1, the new car was demonstrated to the mayor and aldermen of the City. At the corner of Baker & Ward Streets, Mayor L.H. Choquette, Aldermen A.S. Horswill, Ross Fleming & J.P. Morgan, City Electrical Engineer J.P. Coates, City Clerk W.E. Wasson and T.G. Parker boarded the car . . . [which] was in charge of George Hall, Superintendent of the electrical railway. With him were H. Bellis, conductor, and L[es] Hall, [who later succeeded his father, George, as superintendent], car barn employee. The car made a complete trip around the system with the mayor and the aldermen on board. At Fairview the excellent fender, which is the latest design of safety device was demonstrated. The car rounded the new circle recently constructed in Fairview without any difficulty whatsoever. Returning to the city, the car was driven around the hill; it took every hill without any difficulty. After the demonstration, it was put on the regular service and was for the few hours it was on yesterday, crowded with interested citizens.

. . . the car now in operation is of the pay-as-you-enter style and has an entrance only on the right hand side. In order that the service might be the same all through, the other cars on the run will be closed on the left hand side and passengers wishing to board are requested to wait on the right hand side of the car as it approaches . . .

The construction of the loop at Lakeside Park, and the fact that #3 was a single-ended, pay-as-you-enter (PAYE) car spelled the end of #1's and #2's careers as double-ended cars. Until #3's arrival, there had been no loop at Lakeside Park - the crew merely changed ends and went back the way that they had come. Now the two original cars became, at least for operating purposes, single-end cars, although they could still be operated from either end as necessary. One end became the PAYE end, and was marked accordingly.

Affleck describes the impression which the new car made on him as a young child.

. . . [I] can remember well as a small child of 3 or 4 years being fascinated by the coke heater in the vestibule which was used

Conductor Harold Bellis, circa 1914

to heat the car. The coke heater was located on the left-hand side of the front vestibule. A fan forced hot air along a primitive duct which ran under the seats on the left hand side of the car. Passengers electing seats on the left side were toasted; those on the right side froze. The other cars sported electric heaters under the seats, and were *murder* on rubbers. Car #3 also had an open front vestibule which permitted small-fry to observe the motorman working the controls . . .

The smell of the burning coke was liberally dispensed throughout the car making it a "real stinker". To make up for this, the car was a very fast runner.[14]

As intended, the new car served as a spare. Prior to its arrival, the schedule allowed for each of the other cars to be available for maintenance on a daily basis. This worked well for routine upkeep, but not when major repairs were involved. The third car and the efforts of a

Car #23 takes on passengers at Lakeside Park.

Car #22 (formerly #2) displaying its original safety fender and a new coat of paint

dedicated group of street railwaymen kept what was essentially an obsolete group of cars operating through the coming difficult days of the Second World War right to the end of service in 1949.

Affleck also suggests that prior to 1930 the addition of #3 permitted a twenty minute service "... chiefly on Wednesday, Saturday and Sunday afternoons in summer. One car would wait above the Stanley and Latimer belt line turn-off until the upbound car had turned along Latimer. *Day-trippers* from Trail used to swell the Wednesday, Saturday and Sunday population in the summer. Stores closed Wednesday afternoons in summer in Nelson, and I think also in Trail. Various organizations would charter the *Kuskanook* or the *Moyie* for a Wednesday afternoon excursion up the

West Arm. Lesser organizations would stage a Wednesday afternoon picnic in Lakeside Park. As the depression progressed, Wednesday afternoon excursions diminished, while Wednesday afternoon picnics increased." On summer afternoons during the depression years, if the cars and the generating equipment were up to it, the carbarn maintenance crew would also take #3 out at five-o'clock during the last hour of their shift to make it possible for wage earners leaving work on Baker Street to find room on an uphill-bound car at about 5:20 p.m.

He recalls another advantage of having a third car at events such as "the windup of the Anglican Sunday School picnic in July, 1930. Not only did the Proctor excursion steamer *Kuskanook* berth at the Nelson City Wharf beside the *Nasookin crow boat* on that hot summer evening, but all three streetcars of the Nelson Street Railway idled at the corner of Front and Hall Streets awaiting the boarding of homeward-bound excursion passengers. To a six-year old boy, this indeed represented the *big time* in public transportation"[15]

Having grown up in Nelson during the streetcar era,

Downtown office workers hurry to board #22 on Baker Street

Affleck is able to describe something of the social impact of this means of transportation in the early years of the century.

Prior to World War I, few Nelson residents kept a horse and carriage or an automobile. The more affluent could hire a cab, but most who attended the rink, the roller-skating rink, or the opera house relied on the streetcar to take them home after an evening out. In the twenties and thirties, the movie theatres usually disgorged their *late-show* patrons just in time for them to catch the *last car* home. On Sunday afternoons in the summer, the streetcars would be crowded with entire families from uphill who, laden with picnic impedimenta, would catch the car for Lakeside Park. Fairview students bound for junior high school or the old high school packed the street car in the morning, particularly in winter. The truly venturesome student would tear home to Fairview on foot in the noon hour, wolf down some lunch, then catch the streetcar back to school. In late February and March, walking in Nelson tends to be particularly treacherous, as the heavy run-off

Paddlewheel steamer *Nasookin* up on the ways at the C.P.R. shipyard

during the few hours around noon turns quickly to glare ice as soon as the sun slips over the mountain. Housewives accordingly patronized the streetcar. My mother claimed the 5-cent streetcar ride up the hill was a very cheap form of insurance against falls and fractures, a view which I am sure was supported by many other women who struggled on those slippery streets during inclement weather ... In winter automobiles tended to drive on the streetcar tracks. This practice, particularly during the quick-thaw, sudden-freeze period at the end of the winter made for snowpack which occasionally caused spectacular derailments. The Latimer and Hendryx corner, located near the old high school, was a highly susceptible corner. For some reason it seemed to be the rear truck which would derail and wander over to the curb. Cedar Street was a fertile bed for derailments in spring as the frost heave caused the rails to spread.

In the twenties and thirties, it was not necessary to own a watch in order to keep track of time. The CPR yard mounted the whistle from the old *Kokanee* and blew it at noon hours, at changing shift times, etc. At other times of the day, it was the squeal of the streetcar negotiating a sharp turn and the whine of the motor as it climbed the hill which provided a time prompt. On a lazy spring afternoon when the windows in the high school classrooms were open, the squeal of the street-car negotiating the turn up Stanley from Baker at 3:20 p.m. could be heard clearly.* The five minutes of whining up Stanley and Latimer streets were music to the ears of any pupil, because it presaged the end of the school day at 3:30 p.m. I have always had a fairly well-developed sense of pitch. In my school days I could distinguish the high-pitched whine of an approaching #21 from the medium pitch of #22 and the low pitch of #23.[16]

In 1935 the city built a new auditorium on Vernon Street. To allow better access to the new facility, it was proposed that the street railway line be extended one block along Baker Street from Josephine to Hall Street, down Hall Street a distance of one block to Vernon, and back one block along Vernon to Josephine, bringing the tracks within half a block of the new centre. As part of the plan the rails on Josephine were to be taken up, but

*The *squeal* referred to is the inevitable result of steel wheels running on steel track, particularly when the wheel flanges are forced against the rail on tight curves.

Nelson Street Railway, Cars 21 and 22, at Fairview loop, July 19, 1935

From left to right: Mayor J.P. Morgan, Alderman Frank Slater, Roy Sharp, Superintendent A.C. (Les) Hall, J. Jackman, Al Langille, Fred Dalrymple, J.H. Lemmon, Jack Robison, George Fletcher, Jim Joy, Bert Rowley, D.C. Bunce.

For a similar photograph taken after World War II , see page 174.

since the distance was so small, the change (first proposed in 1916)[17] was not thought to be worth the expense, especially since consideration was being given to abandoning the system. Instead, Inspector Rae reported in mid-July 1936 that council intended to install the long-discussed passing track on Josephine Street between Baker and Vernon by the end of August. Unfortunately, this change never did take place.

Snow Problems

In the early 1900s the Nelson area suffered many heavy snowfalls. In 1908, before the arrival of the sweeper, so much snow fell that tramway service had to be suspended. The storm continued for several days, and maintaining operation would have meant digging out the track by hand at heavy expense with little compensating revenue.[18]

Some idea of the snow clearing problems involved in operating the system in the early days have been given by Russell Potter who arrived in Nelson in 1934 to become city engineer. It snowed eight feet that winter, and on one night alone two feet of snow fell. While he kept a bulldozer plowing the tracks, the three streetcars plus the sweeper ran all night long to keep the rails open. He believes that in most of the Pacific Northwest the next morning, Nelson was the only street railway still operating.[19]

In winter, automobiles frequently drove on the streetcar tracks, as this was the only plowed area. The vehicles tended to pack snow into the flangeways of the track causing the streetcars to derail. The problems which snow posed for the little system are further illustrated in the superintendent's timebook which shows that from December 8 to December 31, 1929 the sweeper was out virtually every day.

After Les Hall became superintendent in 1932, whenever an evening snowfall threatened, his wife, Minnie, would tell him to go to bed. She would then stick a broom in the snow outside the house and stay up, watching until the snowfall reached a point on the broom handle which indicated that it was time to call her husband. Les would then call either Charlie Bunce or Jack Robison to help run the sweeper, and out they would go to ensure that the streetcars could operate when morning came.*

Affleck recalls both the Halls (George and Les) and the snow sweeper with obvious admiration.

The Halls lived and breathed street railway. The concept of shift work did not prevail. As a small child, living one-half block from Hendryx Street, I can recall being awakened in the wee sma' hours of the morning by the ghostly sound of the sweeper's brushes dispersing a heavy overnight snowfall. [Mr.] Hall would run the sweeper all night, if the fall of snow was heavy enough, so that the 6:30 a.m. car to Fairview

*A sweeper requires one person to run the car, and the other to operate the controller which drives the big brooms.

Car 21 rounds the curve from Kootenay Street to Hall Mines Road on a wintry day. The carbarn would have been just to the left of this photo.

102

George Hall as a motorman about 1914.

would deliver the CPR shipyard crew on time. They lived in a different world from that which prevails today.

The Hall Family and the Street Railway Tradition

George Hall joined the street railway in 1906 and served as its superintendent from 1924 to 1932. Wilfred Hall recalls his father as a dedicated street railway man. At home, the talk usually revolved around the cars. George and his wife had originally come from Nanaimo, B.C. where he was one of the survivors of the May 3, 1887 coal mine disaster which killed 34 miners. At first thought to be among the fatalities, he was found to be alive and was taken to a nearby boarding house used as a temporary hospital. This is where he met his future wife. George was badly burned in the accident, and one side had been crushed, which made walking both painful and difficult for the rest of his life. From 1897 to about 1906, he worked in the Hall Mines smelter. When he began with the street railway, he worked mostly as a motorman because this involved much less leg activity than would be required of a conductor.

In those days Wilfred and his brother Stan used to take their father his lunch, meeting his car when it stopped at Innis and Stanley Streets. Their father always had them look in the grooves on the floor in case someone had dropped some money. Not surprisingly, someone usually had. Wilfred suspects that their father was the *someone*.

Clara Sutherland, Minnie and Les Hall's daughter, also offers some insight into what it was like living in a streetcar family.

I was eight years old when dad took over the position of superintendent from his father . . . I can remember the pleasure of taking Dad's lunch to him at the carbarn where I'd usually find him climbing the ladder from what appeared to be a 'bottomless' grease pit where he would have been working on the 'under carriage' of the streetcar. The strong scent of grease as I entered the carbarn, and the hustle and bustle of the maintenance crew at work - telling me to 'stand back' in case I fall into that awesome pit - is an experience I shall never forget.

Being a member of a streetcar family was never knowing when the phone was going to ring with one problem or another connected with the streetcar system, such as the time Dave Webster phoned that one of the newly trained conductors had said, "to hell with it" and walked off the job when the trolley jumped the wire, just once too often, at the corner of Stanley and Baker Street leaving Dad with no replacement for him other than himself.

I doubt that any member of the family got much sleep during the winter months, especially when the snow fell the heaviest. It was either Mom calling Dad to get up and get out on the sweeper, at which time he'd phone Charlie Bunce (his right-hand man) and away they would go, or Dad

Superintendent George Hall gives his son Les the money for his change fund on the latter's first day as a conductor. In the background is the family home at 214 Gore Street.

coming in half-frozen from having lain in the snow for hours to put the car back on the track, or from having the sweeper out to clear fresh snow before the first streetcar ran that morning. There was never a dull moment.

I remember the times Dad would sit up until the wee hours of the morning writing out reports, mulling over estimates, or drawing up plans for another necessary piece of equipment such as the welder he designed and built for the line [track] crew. One purpose of this welder was to smooth out the joints between sections of track by building up the rails with welded metal . . .

Being a member of a streetcar family was to feel and show a great deal of respect and admiration towards our Dad whose ingenuity and dedication to his work kept him well occupied, yet he found time to take his family on many enjoyable camping trips where we would sit around the campfire listening to him play the violin, or recite the poems of Robert Service.

Dad's streetcar records were passed on to me in 1981 and later became of great value to Lyle Ward in assisting him with information on the restoration of car 23. It was only after we had read those records that we realized the extent of the hardships encountered to keep the old streetcar system on track . . .

Les and Minnie Hall look over a testimonial to Les' long service to the city of Nelson

It was fortunate that both George and his son Les were very mechanically inclined. After 1914 when the Allis-Chalmers-Bullock firm ceased making streetcar components, the Halls had no choice but to manufacture their own.

Hard Times

The depression of the 1930s inevitably affected the street railway. In an attempt to give the fleet more of a *big city* look, the cars were renumbered: #1 becoming 21; #2, 22; and #3, 23. Despite their new coat of paint, the deterioration in almost every piece of equipment could not be hidden. The generating equipment was seriously in need of major overhaul, and when, after a series of breakdowns, the second generator also failed

The carbarn at Kootenay Street and Hall Mines Road

on August 18, 1937, a bus had to fill in for the powerless cars. The failure of council to provide funds for even minimal maintenance was only too visible to the ratepayers. Following an inspection of the cars and the system, Inspector Rae outlined the repairs which would be required for continued operation. Mayor Stibbs, faced with an estimate of $150,000 to put the system back in shape and buy new cars, tried to convince the public to substitute buses.[20]

On May 17, 1939 the public was asked to make a choice between repairing the street railway or substituting a bus system running on roughly the same route. They voted for the streetcars, 503 to 445, probably believing that council would ". . . let the buses go to wrack and ruin just about as quickly as they had allowed the street railway to deteriorate." As a result, a considerable number of new ties and much new rail was laid in both 1939 and 1940. In addition, the shop staff used considerable ingenuity in overhauling the motors. This expenditure of time and money was most fortunate, since the Second World War soon made any extensive repair work virtually impossible.

Runaway On Stanley Street Hill

While the system continued to have its share of the usual minor derailments, it was spared any major accidents for some twenty years. Its luck ran out on Saturday, October 10, 1942 when #22 (formerly #2 and already involved in two major accidents) ran away down Stanley Street. Owing to the amount of leaves and tree sap on the rails, the brakes failed to hold on the slippery rails. At the corner of Baker and Stanley streets, the car left the track and climbed the sidewalk on the north side of Baker Street. Fortunately there were only three passengers on board when the accident took place at 5:40 p.m. Equally fortunately the street railway had taken out insurance against just such an event some two years before. No one was seriously hurt, although those on board including the car's crew Motorman D.S. Webster and Conductor W.C.

(Scotty) McCandlish, suffered many bruises, sprains, cuts, and scratches.

In his investigation carried out on October 14, Chief Inspector Rae described the accident as follows:

Motorman Webster stated that he had been operating car no. 22 all afternoon and the weather was clear. When going up Stanley Street to Latimer he had no trouble in making stops or in starting the car but in turning at Latimer Street to go around the mountain loop there was a slight drizzle and the wind had gotten up. When returning around the loop to Stanley Street several leaves had blown onto the rails. Also there was considerable sap from the trees that are on both sides of the street. The trees are Maple and Mountain Ash. From Latimer Street for a distance of two blocks to Carbonate Street there is a downgrade of 7 1/2 per cent. From Carbonate to Silica, one block, it is 6 per cent and from Silica Street to Baker Street, a distance of two blocks, it is 10 per cent. In descending this grade Webster was going to make a stop at Silica Street, and when applying the brakes the car began to skid. He released the brakes and applied power to start the wheels revolving. He then applied the brakes and the car began again to skid. The car did not stop but kept descending the grade. He kept releasing the brakes and applying sand to the rails. At the intersection of Stanley and Baker Street there is a sharp curve which leads the tracks onto Baker Street. Webster figures that on reaching the Baker Street curve, the car was travelling about twenty miles an hour with the wheels skidding. When partly around the curve the front wheels left the rails. Baker Street being a paved street, the car headed for the north side of Baker Street. When the rear trucks got about half way on the curve they also jumped the track and the rear end also turned north, the side of the street car colliding with a lamp standard about thirty feet from the front of the car on the left side. The standard was broken off and thrown into the door of the Royal Bank which is on the corner of Stanley and Baker Streets. The back truck climbed the curb and was on the sidewalk when the car was stopped . . .

There were three passengers in the car and you will note from the Doctor's certificates the injuries they received.[21]

One of the three was Sylvia Shorthouse, daughter of

future mayor T.S. Shorthouse. She was ejected from the car through an open window but miraculously escaped any major injury in the process. The mayor insisted that the car crew go to the hospital to be checked. Since no transportation was available, they walked.[22]

After putting #22 back on the track Superintendent Les Hall carefully drove the errant car back to the barn where Rae conducted a thorough examination of it and reported that:

On examining the car at the carbarn the front axle of the rear truck was broken, and all four wheels of that truck were badly skidded [i.e., the wheels now had flat spots on them] and I believe the back axle is also bent. These will require new wheels and axles. The front truck has been sprung to some extent and both trucks will require to be dismantled for inspection and overhaul. The side of the car - the main side sill at the fourth window from the rear of the car on the left side is also fractured [This is like the car's spinal column except that a car has two - one on each side.] and the side of the car staved in. Windows are broken and part of the rear is also smashed in.

I have requested that a new side sill be applied and all the sheeting from the left side of the car be removed in order to examine the bracing and repairing of the window sills and frames. Regarding the roof, this type of car has an upper story [clerestory] and I have recommended that while this car is undergoing repairs the upper story be removed and the roof made into a monitor [actually an arch] or turtle-back roof. This will greatly strengthen the body of the car and also do away with a lot of extra maintenance in taking care of ventilators, windows, and fastenings.[23]

In Rae's report, the slippery conditions on the track and a combination of a badly-worn outside running rail and a worn and badly-spaced guard rail were held to be responsible for the accident rather than the motorman. It was estimated that the car was travelling twenty miles an hour when it derailed, and there was a faint possibility that if the guard rail had been properly placed, it might have made the corner as had happened in the December 6, 1900 incident. The major problem was

A TRIP AROUND THE NELSON STREET RAILWAY ON CAR 21

0 = point from which the corresponding photograph was taken

Car 21 turns onto Innes Street after its long climb up Cedar 6

Two girls board #21 on Nelson Avenue

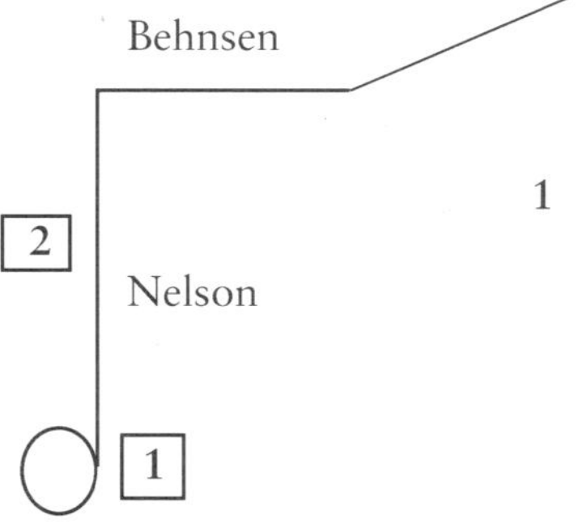

Car 21 at Lakeside Park

110

Looking down Innes Street from Cedar. Note the desolate nature of the area even as Nelson nears the end of the streetcar era in 1949.

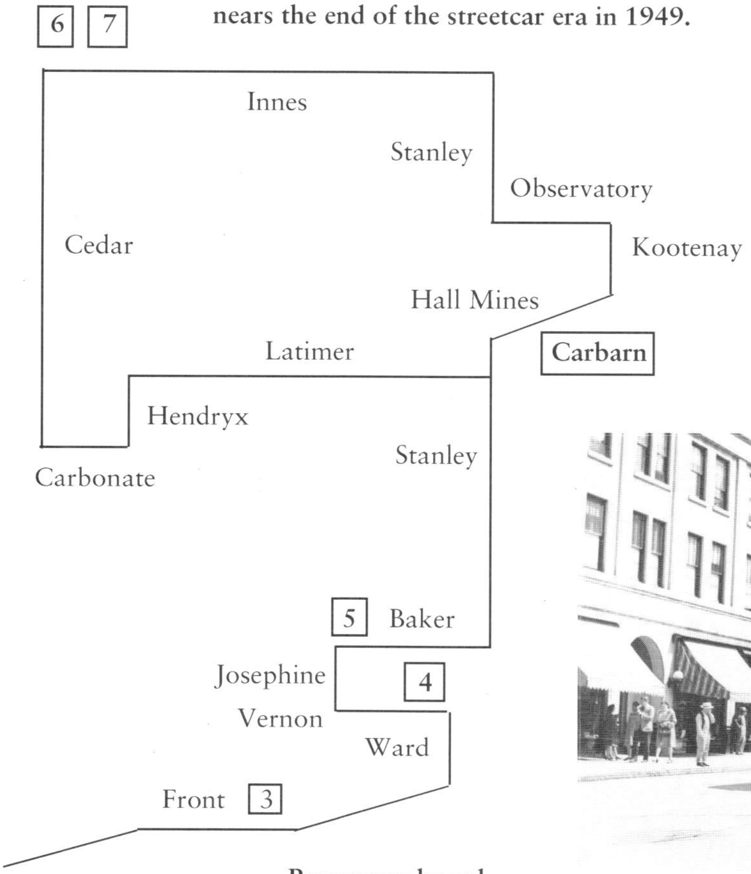

7

Passengers board #21on Baker Street

5

Cars 21 and 22 meet at the passing track on Front Street at Hall

3

4

Car 21 heads toward Josephine Street after turning onto Vernon Street from Ward. John Houston's monument is behind the car.

that owing to sap and fallen leaves on the track, the rail
was extremely slippery. As a precaution against similar
difficulties in the future, Rae recommended that cars
apply sand while going *up* the hill so that the rail would
be prepared to some extent for the trip *down*. He also
outlined the work on the rail which he considered
absolutely essential for the prevention of similar accidents. After a certain amount of pressure on those who
controlled Nelson's purse strings, this was done.

Improvements

The British Columbia Electric Railway had already
embarked on an extensive program to replace the deck
roofs on many of its cars with arch or turtle-back roofs
as part of an extensive re-building and modernization
program designed to give their older cars a more con-
temporary look and could therefore offer their experience to the Nelson staff. Rae took Superintendent Hall
to the B.C. Electric's shops in Vancouver where he
observed the work first hand. Car 22 was completely
rebuilt by December 30, returning to service in January,
1943. The rebuild included converting its roof from the
railway pattern to an arch pattern. Its conversion was
such a success that the same was done with its twin, #21.
The white *teardrop* design which appears on the side of
the cars was added about this time to improve their
visibility, but was removed after the war.

In February, 1944, Superintendent Les Hall reported
to the Department of Railways that a great many
improvements had been made on the system.

Life guards have been put in place of the old type fenders,
heaters have been made and put in the back vestibules which
add much comfort to riding on cars in cold weather. Four
electric heaters were placed in barn pits to prevent air lines
on cars from freezing while standing in barns. Snap switches
have been placed on [the carbarn] wall so that motormen can
turn heat on when [a] car is brought to the barn. Ten electric
lights were placed in the barn pit for inspection work. A
welding machine was also made at the carbarn for miscella-
neous work such as building up track joints, switches, brake

Les Hall trying out the new welding
machine

heads, etc. Two hundred and fifty joints and several brake
heads have been built up. This machine is invaluable to our
work.

Owing to the increased number of passengers being
carried on the cars it is becoming difficult to keep the cars on
schedule. A good deal of time is lost through the inability of
passengers to enter the cars while others are leaving.*
Therefore the front vestibules are being altered to front exits.
The door rigging has already been installed which enables
the motorman to open and close the door without leaving
the controls.[24]

Despite the improvements made to the roadbed and
to the cars, none of them was sufficient to prevent a
repeat of the 1942 accident three years later in 1945.
This time, the official reports indicate that it was the
motorman who was to blame.

Repeat Performance on Stanley Street

On July 22, 1945 #22 was taken out of the carbarns for
the afternoon service. As was mentioned earlier, the
practice at that time was for one car to begin the daily
service at 6:00 a.m. It would continue until it came to
the carbarn on the 10:00 a.m. run when passengers and
crew would change over to the other car which had
been receiving servicing during the early morning.[25]
Car 22 would have been taken out of service at 10:00
a.m., and worked on until it was added to the afternoon

* Until this was done, passengers entered and left only by the rear doors.
After the change, passengers continued to board at the rear of the car, but
could exit at the front.

schedule for the ill-fated trip.

When the car was taken out of the barn, its air gauge showed the required 60-pounds pressure. At the subsequent inquiry, the motorman on the previous shift stated that he had not encountered any problems with the car's brakes. The car had been taken up the hill to the terminus at Stanley and Innes streets to re-enter service; the controls were changed and the car began its trip back down. After stopping near the carbarn to allow the *up* car to swing onto Latimer, the motorman started down Stanley Street. The account is continued in

Car 22 at the end of its wild trip down Stanley Street

A close-up view of the damage

the report of J. H. Short, acting chief inspector of the Department of Railways who had replaced William Rae on the latter's retirement.

[After] about one or two blocks . . . he made an attempt to apply the brake to pick up a passenger but found the brake did not respond and noticed that the pressure gauge did not show any pressure in the main reservoir. He moved the reverse handle to reverse position and applied the power controller to the second notch then to power off several times . . . He did not attempt to use the handbrake and he did not notice whether the air compressor switch was turned on or off . . . [26]

The car left the rails at Stanley and Baker and ran for about half a block down Stanley badly damaging three cars and a heavy freight truck belonging to Reubin

Buerge, knocked down a telephone pole, and finally came to rest at the rear entrance of Hood's Bakery at the mouth of the alley between Baker and Vernon Streets. Fortunately there were no passengers on board. Using block and tackle, two city trucks were able to pull #22 back on to the tracks. By 8:00 p.m. the car had returned to the carbarn under its own power.[27] Short described the damage to the car as follows:

I made an inspection of the car and was given to understand that nothing had been touched since the accident. The front vestibule was quite badly damaged and the center sills were splintered and also the main frames and truck frames sprung. In making an examination of the air brake equipment I found the compressor governor pipe had a new break on one side of the air strainer and the pipe on the other side of the strainer had an old crack in it. This probably would leak some but not enough to cause any trouble. All the other air brake equipment was intact. The brake system, was charged up from the air compressor and a test of the equipment made. The piston travel was checked and found to be standard 8-inch. The foundation brake gear was checked and found in good working order and no fouling of the levers could be noticed. The braking power was calculated and found to be about 104 per cent of the light weight

Car 22 on Baker Street following rebuilding after the runaway down Stanley. Notice the new roof, the revised paint scheme, and the fact that the car still retains the old safety fender although somewhat modified.

of the car based on 50-pound cylinder pressure which is ample for this equipment. A leakage test was made which showed 2 1/2 pounds leakage in two minutes which is considered good for a car in service.

In the subsequent inquiry it was revealed that the maintenance man at the carbarn had worked on #22 after its morning shift and, following standard practice, shut the compressor off.* Following the accident the switch was found to be still in the *off* position, meaning that once the motorman had made his first few brake applications there was no more air. The motorman was suspended. The Department of Railways recommended that a red light be installed on the cars in front of the motorman which would light up when the air compressor was switched off.

Trolley Buses?

By the end of the 1940s, both the equipment and the track were nearing a condition where replacement would be necessary. Throughout the Second World War, money and manpower for maintenance had been in short supply in all cities. The severe deterioration of street railway systems and the massive expenditure required to repair and upgrade them undoubtedly was a major factor in any decision to convert to buses.

Nelson, too, had to decide about the future of its transportation system. Council commissioned a report by Vancouver consulting engineer A.C.R. Yuill. He stressed that because the cars were built before the First World War, replacement parts were unobtainable. He continued, "The fact that the superintendent and staff have managed to keep up the appearances of the cars does not alter the fact that they are overdue for retirement."[28] Another of his concerns was that the substation was unable to handle the peak loads required on holidays and after performances at the Civic Centre. In conclusion, he recommended that the city convert to trolley buses. As a result of his report, the citizens were asked in 1946 to choose among five transportation options.* While the heaviest vote favoured the purchase of new trolley buses, council stated that the small number of coaches required could not be obtained. (Interestingly, in the same period, Edmonton placed an order for two in 1946, and Kitchener was able to purchase a single bus in 1948.) Thirty per cent of those who voted favoured the purchase of new street cars, but council ignored their wishes, and proposed instead to substitute buses (favoured by only four per cent of the voters). However, for a time, no action was taken.

Judging from the lengthy correspondence between Superintendent Hall and the Ohio Brass Company (and its Canadian subsidiary the Canadian Ohio Brass Company), it would appear that the trolley bus option was still being considered. The company suggested that Hall send them a map of the city as well as a drawing of the carbarn layout, and they would try to design a system for him.

On May 15, 1947, Claude R. Kingsbury, district manager for Canadian Ohio Brass, came to Nelson, and in company with Mayor Waters, W.A. Gordon, city clerk, George C. Wallach, chairman of the street railway committee, and Superintendent Hall surveyed the proposed route by car. In Kingsbury's opinion, the route seemed to be "entirely satisfactory for trolley coach operation." Most of the proposed trolley bus route would be one way except for three blocks on Baker and one on Vernon where trolley coaches would operate in both directions.

Kingsbury provided an estimate for enough overhead wire and fittings to enable a trolley coach coming from the south or hill end of the line to loop over Baker, Hendryx, Vernon and Hall, and then back up the hill. The same loop would also allow a coach coming from the Fairview area to loop downtown without going up the hill thereby allowing only a portion of the system to be operated if this became necessary. He estimated that the total cost of the overhead system including new poles in most areas would be $63,100. Since trolley

---

*The results of the voting were as follows:

1. Repair existing streetcars(13%)
2. Purchase new streetcars (30%)
3. Purchase trolley buses (43%)
4. Purchase gas buses (4%)
5. Leave decision to Council (10%)[29]

coaches use twin overhead wires, one for power feed and the other for return, there would be a further expense of $8,000 to cover the cost of stringing the negative return. With streetcars this function is performed by the rails. To include the necessary overhead and switches for conversion of the existing carbarn would add a further $5,000. The new buses were not included in these estimates, since they would be obtained from a separate source.[30]

On his return from the Canadian Transit Association convention in Banff (June, 1948) Superintendent Hall reported on his activities there to George C. Wallach, chairman of council's street railway committee. Based on Hall's report, the Canadian Ohio Brass Company was asked to prepare an estimate of the cost of building a trolley bus line. The company estimated that the total cost of conversion, including housing of the vehicles, materials and labour (but not the coaches themselves) for the proposed 6-mile line would be $71,650. The route would follow to some extent the old street railway, but would see service extended to

One of Calgary Transit's Brill-built trolley buses waits outside the municipal garage.

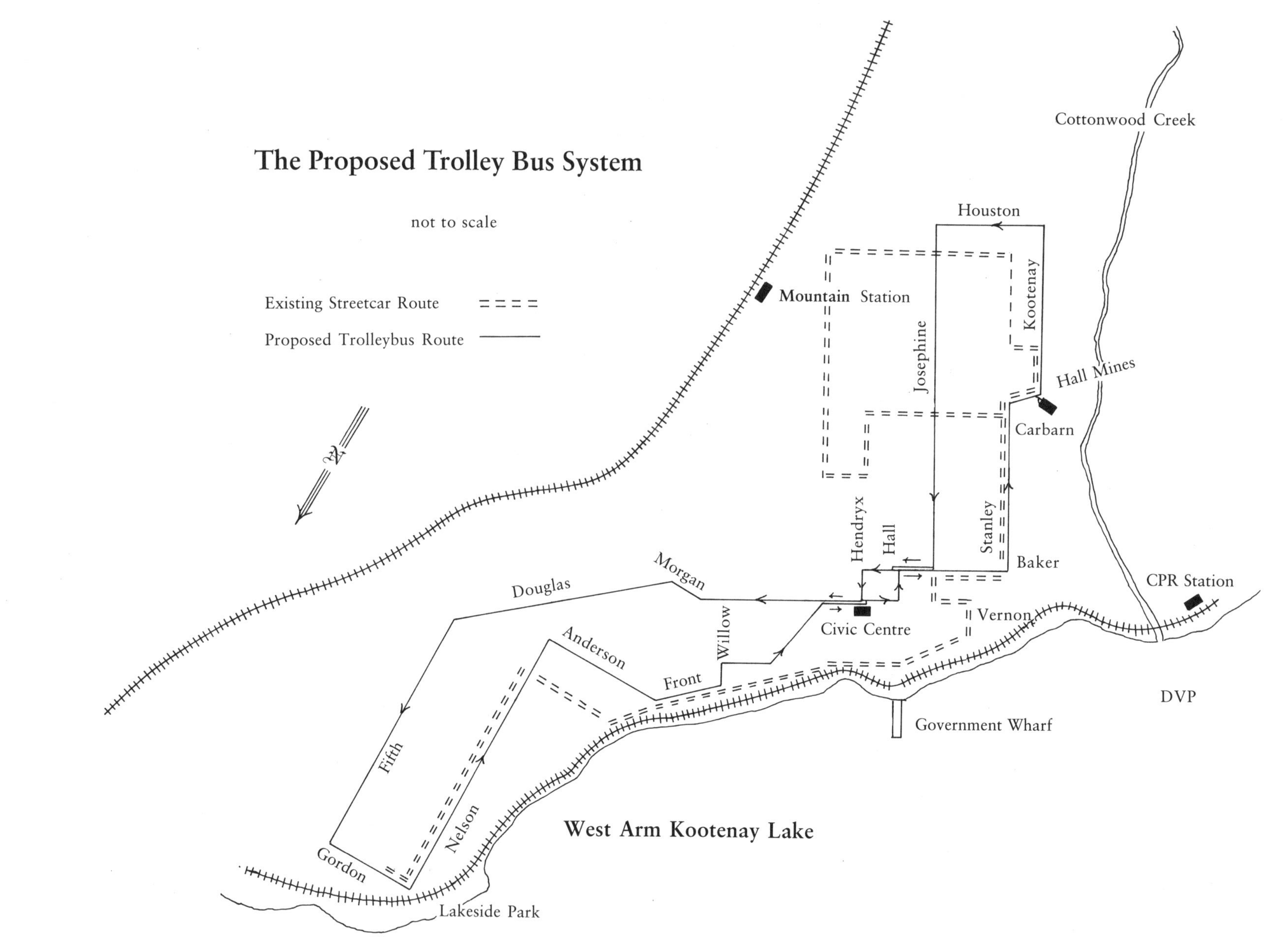
The Proposed Trolley Bus System
not to scale
Existing Streetcar Route
Proposed Trolleybus Route
N
Cottonwood Creek
Houston
Mountain Station
Josephine
Kootenay
Hall Mines
Carbarn
Stanley
Hendryx
Hall
Baker
Morgan
Douglas
Willow
Vernon
CPR Station
Civic Centre
Front
DVP
Government Wharf
Anderson
Fifth
Nelson
Gordon
West Arm Kootenay Lake
Lakeside Park

other areas of the city as well. Fifty per cent of the poles in service on the street railway would be useable by the trolley bus system, necessitating the purchase of a further 350 new wooden poles. The company also included drawings showing how storage facilities for the buses might be laid out.

Council did not look favorably on the report, despite the earlier indication of public support for the trolley bus concept. In view of the amounts quoted, it is not surprising that nothing further was done, at least until the summer of 1948 when the Canadian Ohio Brass Company was asked to submit a second, updated proposal. A public meeting to present the proposal was scheduled for November 19. However, on November 9, Hall wrote to Kingsbury to tell him that the meeting had been cancelled. In his reply Kingsbury indicated that this may have occurred because council wished to use motor buses. He was not optimistic about their success. "Frankly, I imagine the motor buses will attempt to put on a top grade show, but I am afraid that if the City of Nelson goes for that, they will find out that in a year or two condition of the buses will not be so good."[31]

Since the bus systems which eventually replaced the streetcars encountered many of the same financial and operating problems, his concerns seem justified.

The End of the Line

Since new developments in bus design had made gas and diesel-powered buses practical for Nelson's steep hills, Interior Stage Lines, of Trail, B.C., an established bus line in the Kootenay region, submitted an offer to council to provide a non-subsidized service using modern Twin Coach buses. Fares were to be ten cents, three for a quarter, and service was to be increased to twenty minutes. Their offer was accepted, and June, 1949 was projected as the date for the changeover.

Superintendent Les Hall was always a staunch supporter of the streetcars, but he was also very objective about the situation in Nelson in their final days. The ending of a letter which he wrote to George Wallach on April 9, 1949 gives a clear picture of his position on the issue of bus substitution.

. . . it is not my intention to cast any [aspersions on] street railways. Street cars are a great vehicle, and essential in large, thickly populated cities, but due to the vast improvement [and] flexibility of rubber tired vehicles, many small cities, both in Canada and the United States, are putting them in operation to avoid the heavy expenditure which would otherwise be required for track repairs.

The end of streetcar service came at 3:30 p.m., Monday, June 20, 1949 when farewell ceremonies were held on Baker and Ward streets for the beloved street-

Buses take over from the streetcars.

*Mrs.Horswill was the owner of the first fare paid in 1899. It was the ten-cent piece, paid by Dr. Lebeau, which had later been mounted in a gold horseshoe and presented to Captain T.J. Duncan, who wore it on his watch chain for many years. It became the property of his wife, and on her death, was given to Mrs. Horswill.

**There are many parallels between the history of the street railway system and that of the motor buses which replaced them. When the initial bus company declared bankruptcy in the early 1950s, the city took over responsibility for the service. In 1969 it was recommended that the city sell the transit system, since the operation had lost an average of $35,000 per year. Council raised fares to twenty-five cents and cut back the service. Beginning in 1972, the city began to receive an operating grant from the provincial government which solved many of the system's financial problems. Then in April, 1975, a fire in the municipal garage destroyed three of the buses. Fortunately the city was able to obtain buses from the now provincially-owned fleet, and full service was restored after three days. The service is now a part of the province-wide B.C. Transit operations with costs being split between B.C. Transit and the city.[33]

cars. On hand were three people who had ridden on the first car in 1899: Mrs. A.T. Horswill,* Mr. W. Duncan, and Mr. T.C. Duncan (manager and secretary in 1899-1900), the last two, officers of the original company. At 4:06 p.m. the first bus started on its way, and street railway service in Nelson came to an end.**

A very poignant commentary on the final ceremony was contributed by Les Hall in a letter to the author.

The day the buses took over the Street Railway will remain in my memory to the end of time. While the cameras took pictures of the buses and their operators, on Baker at Ward Street, the street cars and their crews stood on the tracks beside them looking quite smart but receiving little attention after all the years of faithful service.[32]

Cars 21 and 22 were stored in the loop at the park in Fairview for almost two years after their replacement by the buses. For a time there was a proposal that they be placed in Lakeside Park, one as a shelter and the other as the nucleus of a museum, by members of the newly-formed Kootenay Historical Association. Eventually, the cars were taken off their trucks, loaded on a flatbed, and taken three miles out along the lake where one became a workshed and the other a summer cottage. At some later date they were dismantled and burned.

Their mate, #23, fared somewhat better. For a time it was used as a skating shelter in a playground at Delbruck and Falls streets, but was soon subjected to vandalism In 1951 it was sold to Mr. and Mrs. J. J. Carney of the North Shore. The sweeper was taken to a Boy Scout camp on the Ymir Road where it survived until it was burned in the 1970s. The carbarn was used for several years by city work crews as a storage shed, but a gas station is now located on its site.

As for the line's employees, eleven of them spent the period from August 6 to August 30 taking up the track. The last entry in Superintendent Hall's paybook is for October 15, 1949 when a small group of employees

cleaned up the carbarn for the last time. As they left, locking the door behind them, it is doubtful that any of them believed that streetcars would ever run again in Nelson.

Cars 21 and 22, their trucks and other equipment removed, wait at Lakeside Park for the last time.

Part Two

1980 to 1992

During the past decade, there has begun
a movement throughout North America
to rescue what is left of our street railway
heritage, a heritage which was so lightly
thrown away in the 1940s and 1950s.

Chapter Six

PRESERVATION   1980-1989

Preserving A Heritage

THE CITY OF NELSON provides a perfect setting for historical restoration and preservation. The abandonment of railway passenger service to the city, and the construction of the Salmo-Creston highway which distanced the city from the main provincial highway system virtually guaranteed that the wanton destruction of heritage structures which characterized other centres driven by *development* would not take place in Nelson. The result is that much of the city remains as it was in the early part of the century. Nelson has capitalized on its heritage. Plaques, brochures describing walking tours, and the restoration of many buildings along Baker Street all reflect a community will to keep what was important from the old days. The desire to preserve one of the community's former streetcars is a logical part of this movement.

Car 23 Is Rescued

When #23 was taken out of service after the end of streetcar service in 1949, it was used for a time as a skating rink shelter at Delbruck and Falls Street.[1] As mentioned at the end of the previous chapter, it was then purchased by Mr. and Mrs. J. J. Carney for use as a dog kennel. They moved the car to a site on Nasookin Road on the north shore of the West Arm of Kootenay Lake. A three-inch concrete floor was poured inside, and square holes were cut along one side as exits from the various dog pens. Later, the car and the property were acquired by Lloyd and Pat Galbraith. In 1957, #23 was moved 300 yards toward the highway and positioned beside the forward saloon and wheelhouse which had been salvaged from the paddlewheeler *Nasookin*. There, the two *beached* transportation relics served for several years as a museum and craft shop. It is unlikely the tourists and local residents who purchased postcards showing the car beside the remains of the veteran paddlewheeler ever thought they might one day ride that same streetcar along the waterfront in Nelson.

The return of #23 to operation in Nelson probably began on August 18, 1980 when Reid Henderson, administrator of the regional district of Central Kootenay, wrote a letter to the mayor suggesting that, "If the city of Nelson is interested - for heritage development and aesthetic reasons - I understand the *Nasookin* ship bridge and the old streetcar (both located at 4 mile) are up for sale . . . ." A note on the same letter suggests that it was referred to the heritage advisory committee ". . . with the recommendation that consideration be given to approaching the owner with a view to having the articles donated to the city."

Unfortunately, an offer to purchase the property had already been made. Nevertheless, the city administrator, Doug Ormond wrote to Pat Galbraith on September 25, 1980 as follows:

The matter of the sale of the *Nasookin* shipbridge and streetcar was discussed by the city of Nelson Heritage Advisory Committee. That Committee has shown a great interest in acquiring the two items and has recommended to council that every effort be made to purchase them (which recommendation was accepted by council).

However it is our understanding that you wish to honor a commitment to a prior interested party should they wish to proceed with the purchase.

We would be pleased to discuss the possible purchase with you and perhaps you could indicate to us the asking price for these items.

On October 28, the lawyer for the Galbraith estate advised the city that the earlier commitment had expired and that the city should feel free to make whatever offers it wished.[2] Council's reaction was to send Robert G. Adams, director of works and services, to examine the two items.[3] In his report to Ormond dated December 2, 1980, Adams reported that:

Both the ship bridge and street car have deteriorated and would be very expensive to rebuild. We have estimated that between $15,000 and $17,500 would be required to rebuild the Nasookin Bridge. Street Car #23 could be rebuilt for $4,500 and could maybe be used for the 'Bus Stop Shelter'

The wheelhouse and forward saloon of the paddlewheeler *Nasookin* with #23 in use as a craft shop

proposed for Baker Street.* To move the ship bridge we would have to move it to the water and barge it to Lakeside Park. An ideal site would be at Lakeside Park and perhaps it could be converted to use as a concession stand . . .

Adams also had been advised by the real estate firm handling the property that it had received another offer to purchase. Probably on the basis of Adam's report, Ormond advised the law firm that the city was not in a position to purchase the two items.[4]

However, in a letter to Dr. N. E. Morrison and the members of the Heritage Advisory Committee written on February 25, 1981, Margaret Schmidt quoted William Vander Zalm, Minister of Municipal Affairs in the provincial government (later premier of the province), to the effect that, ". . . the downtown revitalization program would fund the purchase of artifacts such as the old streetcar on Mrs. Galbraith's property." Suggesting that this might be one approach to preserving some of Nelson's early history without cost to the city, she urged the committee to recommend to council that ". . . the Downtown Core Committee look into the purchase and restoration of the streetcar and the sternwheeler bridge through the Downtown Revitalization Program . . . " a recommendation which council accepted.[5]

Merv Coles, the new owner of the property on which the *Nasookin's* saloon and wheelhouse and #23 were located, was willing to donate the streetcar to the city in return for an official receipt for tax deduction purposes. Wray Suffredine, executive director of the Nelson Chamber of Commerce, informed council that his members were interested in the project and willing to proceed with it. Suggestions for the car included using it as a tourist information booth or incorporation of the vehicle into the Baker Street project.[6]

The Chamber also requested that the public works department of the city be authorized to offer technical assistance with the understanding that any expenditure

*This project involved the construction of a bus shelter on Ward Street at Baker next to Woolworth's store.

130

of city funds would require council approval. While some members of council were in favour of the project, one alderman was concerned that this initial proposal would result in further requests for city funds, while another expressed doubts about the city's ability to store the car while its restoration proceeded.[7] The proposal was tabled pending examination of the car.

The same day Suffredine wrote to the mayor and council stressing that his previous letter had been misunderstood, and that all council was being asked to do was issue a receipt. The Chamber would take the responsibility for restoration and location.

On August 26, a group which included Alderman Howard Dirks (later the local member of the legislature and ultimately a cabinet minister in the provincial government), Bob Adams, the director of works and services, and Arvid Schneider, the building inspector,

Brill C-36 city bus about to turn onto Baker Street in 1974

examined the car. Schneider described the car's condition as follows:

The under side of the car appears to be in fairly sound condition. It has been sitting on piers approximately two feet high. Wheels and wheel frames, etc. are missing. The rear is in fair to poor condition. The front shows much deterioration although it could probably be restored.

The right side is in fair to poor condition. All windows appear to be old house windows, longer than those on left side. Nearly all framing, or trim, around windows would probably need to be replaced. It appears some of the original side metal is still on the right side.

The left side is completely gone. The lower portion has been replaced with shiplap which has rotted. Many of the wall studs [pillars] are rotted away. The window frames on this side are smaller than on the other; they may be the original size.

The roof is covered with red roofing and seems to keep the water out, certainly not the original material.

The interior floor is covered with 2-3 inches of concrete which would require removal before moving the car. All interior walls have been lined with a thin hardboard type material; none of the original walls seem to be visible.

Car 23's body before being brought to Nelson for restoration

132

Schneider suggested that before moving the car, all non-original material be removed, and the weak areas strengthened. In his report to the city administrator, Adams was concerned that the city did not have a storage site where the car could be protected from further deterioration.[8] He offered, however, to provide whatever technical assistance the Chamber requested.[9]

At the council meeting of September 20, 1982, Alderman Dirks (seconded by Alderman Ruth O'Bryan) moved that council advise the Chamber that it was willing to accept the car as a donation, ". . . provided however it is clearly understood that all costs of moving, storage and restoration are to be borne by the Chamber from funding outside of that contributed yearly by this council, this offer subject to the Chamber of Commerce taking ownership of the streetcar for the sum of $1.00."[10] There seemed to be some concern about the provisions of the Income Tax Act with respect to donations, and the motion was tabled. Concern was also expressed by at least one alderman that the Chamber might not be willing to accept the car, once the city had obtained it, and the city would be stuck with it.[11]

The British Columbia Ministry of Municipal Affairs then advised council that a formal appraisal of the car would have to be made before a tax receipt could be issued. Furthermore, if the city became the owner of the car, the transfer to the Chamber would have to conform to the Municipal Act respecting disposal of municipal assets which included public posting of the sale (in effect allowing anyone to bid on the car). At the same time, since the Chamber was presumably not registered in Ottawa as a charitable organization, it could not issue the receipt itself.[12]

When it had taken all of these problems into consideration, council passed the following resolution, "That the city do not accede to the request from the Chamber of Commerce to issue a receipt to the owner of Street Car No. 23 . . . for income tax purposes if possession is taken of the structure by the Chamber."[13]

Work Begins On Restoration

Since the business of a tax receipt seemed to have reached an impasse,* Merv Coles, while retaining title, released the car for restoration purposes to a consortium comprising the Chamber of Commerce and the Vocational Division of Selkirk College. The principal of the Vocational Division, Bruce Meldrum, played a major role in #23's subsequent restoration.

To cover the initial costs of restoring the car, the Nelson Chamber of Commerce and the Vocational Division of Selkirk College applied jointly for a Federal government community development grant. Several Nelson residents who remembered streetcars with affection or who were interested in streetcars in general formed the Committee for the Restoration of Car 23, one of whose major forces was the late Lyle Ward. Ward was very much involved in automobile restoration, and brought some unique skills to the project, not the least of which was his commitment to the project and his ability to uncover photographs of the cars and of the system itself. The author enjoyed a fairly lengthy correspondence with Lyle beginning early in 1983 as the latter tried to find sources for the various components which #23 would require in its restoration. Ward concluded his letter to the author of February 25, 1983 with the comment, ". . . work is still progressing and we are now trying to find ways of getting public support of [the] project, so some day the city will want it back on tracks again." This commitment to seeing the return of streetcar service in Nelson, repeated again in other correspondence, is one of the reasons why the new carbarn in the city is named in his honour. Regrettably, Lyle did not live to see the final restoration of #23.

The car was moved to an indoor facility at the college in November 1982 where rotted wood and metal parts were removed after being carefully photographed and catalogued. New side posts were built and structural steel members were replaced where necessary. The project was funded as a federal government Commu-

Lyle Ward

*Later, when the Nelson Electric Tramway Society was formed, this group, as a non-profit organization, was in a legal position to provide Coles with such a receipt, and title to the car was turned over to them by him.

134

nity Development job creation project which lasted until March, 1983.[14]

The work was carried out in several stages depending on the Canada Works grants received. The second grant of $26,000 received in January 1984 permitted the structural work to be finished; new steel exterior plates to be installed on the body; new vestibules constructed; window frames and sashes to be built; a new subfloor installed; the exterior painted, and a new roof covering put on. From the funds received as part of the third grant seats were constructed; windows, a hardwood floor, and interior panelling were installed, and the necessary wiring took place.[15]

For a time the possibility of using electrical equipment and trucks from Toronto PCC streetcars was considered, and the project went so far as to secure

Car 23 under cover at Selkirk College's Rosemont campus. Restoration has begun, and the new pillars show the amount of work involved.

Toronto Transit Commission's PCC #4504 and, with
the help of Selkirk College, bring it to Nelson. Later,
once the possibility of obtaining more authentic trucks
from Europe was explored, the idea of using PCC parts
was abandoned. The PCC trucks were later traded to
the Edmonton Radial Railway Society in exchange for
various electrical and mechanical components needed
for #23 as well as a streetcar frame on which to build
another car.

To raise additional money for the project, the Chamber of Commerce produced a very attractive 1985
calendar which was to be both a tribute to streetcar #23
and a fund-raising venture for its restoration. The
calendar contained brief histories of #23 and of the
street railway in Nelson. Photographs for each month
featured #23 on some part of the Nelson system. A
second, and very successful approach to fundraising

Interior rebuilding underway

was the *seat project*. Lyle Ward found an original seat, had patterns made from which replicas for the restored car were cast, and then sought sponsors for each seat.

Interest In An Operating Street Railway Begins

During the past decade, there has begun a movement to rescue what is left of our street railway heritage, a heritage so lightly thrown away in the 1940s and 1950s. With little or no information on how to go about restoring the abandoned hulks of former streetcars and building a street railway on which to run them, interested groups face a formidable challenge. Projects of this kind in Edmonton, Calgary, Montreal and Guelph, Ontario have seen the restoration of streetcar service albeit in a museum or historical park setting. With restoration of #23's body well underway, interest in Nelson now changed from simply restoring the car to seeing it operate again.

The Baker Street Proposal

The initial plan for street railway operation had been to run the car as a shuttle service along Baker Street in the downtown area. A more ambitious proposal is shown on page 138. In this scheme, the car would operate from a carbarn in the CPR yards, up to Baker Street, along Baker to Hendryx Street, over to Vernon Street, and down Vernon to the four-way stop located at the south end of Baker Street. The car would travel in the right-hand lane with the flow of traffic.

Perhaps the best analysis of the proposal is provided in a memorandum submitted to the mayor and council by the city treasurer, Lloyd Mosely.[16] Mosely believed that in general council supported the concept of returning an operating streetcar to the downtown area. In his letter he pays tribute to the energetic committee of the Chamber (spearheaded by Howard Dirks), but feels that council should have some input into the project. He mentions three specific concerns:

In 1987, #23 (or at least a miniature version of it) appeared on stage in Nelson in an original musical entitled, *I've Always Wanted To Ride A Streetcar* by James Hoffman and Paul Crawford. The miniature version became the feature piece in the information centre which the Society's members later set up in Chahko-Mika Mall during the construction of the lakefront street railway in 1990.

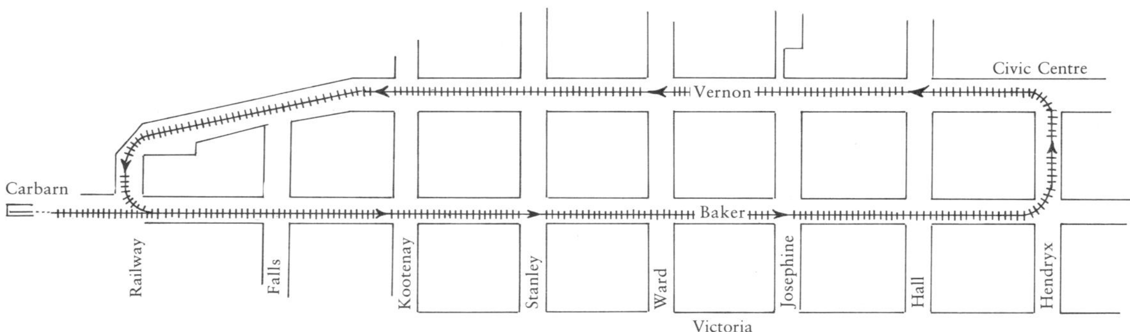

a) Where is the streetcar going to operate?

b) Is the wiring for the streetcar to be overhead or under-
ground (particularly if it operates on Baker Street)?

c) How is construction and operation to be financed?

He then offers some practical suggestions for financing the project.

The city could assist the financing (and perhaps should, as
obviously the operational responsibility and costs will eventually be the City's) of the construction. Some suggestions
are that part of the costs for the Baker Street portion, could
be absorbed in the underexpenditure of the downtown core
rejuvenation (if the merchants agree). The mall could be
approached to share in the costs, and a specified area by-law
could be initiated for this purpose, to spread the costs over
a number of years. The city could apply for assistance
through TIDSA [Tourism Industry Development Subsidiary
Agreement - a provincial government funding program].
There is also approximately $50,000 in Transit Capital
Funds that could be provided.

Early in February, 1986 the Chamber of Commerce
approached council again - this time to enlist its support
in the Chamber's investigation of sources of funding for
a feasibility study to examine the use of #23 in some
type of operation. Since completion of the car, at least
insofar as its body was concerned, was expected for

later in 1986,[17] council approved in principle the Chamber's application for government funding to have a feasibility study carried out.[18]

In indicating its support to the Chamber, council suggested, ". . . the Nelson & District Chamber of Commerce be requested to include the proposal of the Heritage Streetcar #23 operating on the Nelson waterfront as proposed in the Nelson Waterfront Development Plan, in the Feasibility Study for the overall operation of the Streetcar."[19] The proposal which Dirks then submitted on behalf of the Chamber to the Ministry of Industry and Small Business Development in Victoria set the parameters for the street railway that was ultimately constructed. In the proposal three operating locations are envisaged:

a) Baker and Vernon Streets
b) Lake frontage within the city limits, or
c) A combination of both a) and b) "with a connecting link thus tying in downtown development with present and future development along the waterfront."*

The first approach, to the federal and provincial governments (mentioned above), was rejected because the proposal did not meet the criteria for financial support under the Industry Support Program on the grounds that proposals could only be submitted by "B.C. Tourism Associations, individual tourism operators or local regional governments."[20] Despite this initial rejection, Bob Brisco, the member of parliament for Kootenay West, suggested that Dirks inquire whether the regional District of Central Kootenay or the Kootenay Country Tourism Association would be prepared to sponsor the proposal. He also offered to give what help he could.[21]

At this point the Nelson city council stepped in, offering to be the sponsoring body for the proposal. Council's submission does not seem to have had any better reception than the earlier one submitted by the

*As of July 1, 1992, the waterfront component (Phase I) is in operation, and the Baker/Vernon component in a modified form is being considered for Phase II.

Chamber. There were some important developments, however. The Chamber, realizing that the city had to have major input into the streetcar project if it was to share in the project's costs, advised council on February 6, 1987 of the Chamber's intention , ". . . to bring to completion the restoration of Streetcar #23 to a status of public display and kindly request that city council prepare for public display of the Streetcar at the city's own expense. Furthermore the Board (of the Chamber) is willing to work co-operatively with council on any aspect of the Car but realizes that the city needs full licence on the Streetcar if it is going to take fiscal and planning responsibility for the next step in its future."[22]

The city had set aside $5,000 for a feasibility study for the streetcar project, but this was conditional on the provincial government providing a similar amount. When the province was unwilling to provide the neces-

Car 23 getting final touches before being moved to the display facility at Front and Hall streets

sary funds, council advised the Chamber that it could not participate in the study.[23]

Car 23 Returns to Front and Hall Streets

Fortunately the Chamber was awarded a provincial Job Trac grant in the amount of $104,000 to complete the project and place the car on display. Master carpenter John Corbin was appointed as supervisor of this last stage, one which would see ten unemployed workers learn new skills from Selkirk College instructors Don Getty (woodwork) and Roy Crutchley (millwork). One immediate goal of this aspect of the project was to build a display facility for the car in a location which would make the car more visible to the local population. The building would be pre-fabricated at the college, then taken to the display site and erected.[24]

The location chosen for the display facility was historically important. The new building would be erected on land provided by the city on the southeast corner of Hall and Front streets, the site of the passing track which appears in some of the photographs contained in this work. In addition to providing a temporary carbarn for #23, the building would also function as an information centre. Council approved the choice of site early in October.[25]

On February 2nd, the car was moved from Selkirk College into its new quarters. The new facility was officially opened on Saturday, February 13, 1988, enabling many people in Nelson to see the streetcar for the first time.[26] In the first six weeks of its operation, some 1700 people passed through the new centre.

The display facility at Hall and Front
streets while under construction

Chapter Seven

STREETCARS RETURN TO THE KOOTENAYS   1989 -

The Nelson Electric Tramway Society

THE RESTORATION OF #23 was not the only memorable event to take place in Nelson in the late 1980s. The city was chosen as the locale for the filming of the feature motion picture, *Roxanne*, starring Darryl Hannah and Steve Martin, while the Nelson area was selected as a site for the British Columbia Winter Games held in 1989. In addition, the restoration of many of the buildings along Baker Street as part of the Downtown Revitalization Program did much to enhance the strong community feeling for which the area has been known from its earliest days. This spirit worked to the advantage of the streetcar project. Just as the Nelson of the 1890s saw no reason why it should not share in street railway development along with Vancouver and other large cities to the south, so the Nelson of a hundred years later was willing to support the construction of a vintage street railway similar to the projects already in place in Calgary and Edmonton.

With #23 on display and once more visible to the city's residents, the emphasis changed from restoring a car to bringing one back to operation. An important first step in achieving this goal was the incorporation of the Nelson Electric Tramway Society on June 12, 1988, with Dr. Mike Culham as its first president.* When the focus of the project shifted to operation rather than simple exhibition, the Chamber recognized that management of such a large undertaking demanded the creation of a separate organization. A great deal had already been achieved in arranging for the preservation and restoration of the car. Now it would be up to the Nelson Electric Tramway Society to build the street railway on which it would run.

The new group, which decided to use the name of the first Nelson street railway in its title, had two major goals:

1. To collect and disseminate information [on] the street railway history of Nelson, thereby preserving this portion of our city's heritage.

2. To get streetcar 23 back on track again.[1]

One of the first steps in the achievement of the second goal took place at a ceremony held at the display facility on December 7, 1988 when Allen Early, President of the Chamber of Commerce, presented to the new group title to the facility as well as various streetcar-related artifacts which it had collected.[2]** Car 23 became the society's property in June, 1991.

Lakeside Route Chosen

The group wasted no time in tackling its objectives. On March 13, 1989, Culham wrote to council describing the society's plans for a waterfront route running from Lakeside Park to the foot of Hall Street. The existing display facility was to be moved to a site near the soccer field. Culham offered the society's rationale for this decision.

The Society believes that the Lakeside route is the least costly and non-contentious course and will not impede either vehicular or pedestrian traffic. It is noted that the Lakeshore route is identified as part of the Nelson Waterfront Development Plan.

*The original streetcar committee had been inactive since Lyle Ward's death in 1986. The Chamber reactivated the Streetcar #23 Committee in January, 1987 with Dr. Michael Culham, a local dentist, as chairman. The Chamber, along with Selkirk College, jointly sponsored #23's restoration.

Dr. Michael Culham

**One more historical artifact surfaced early in 1989. The city donated to the society what is believed to be the last remaining power pole to have carried the street railway's overhead wires. The pole, still in use, was located on Front Street (close to Ward) near the Kinsmen Health Building.[3]

The Society has studied costs of operation and has concluded that ongoing operating and maintenance costs can be achieved by revenue generated from nominal riders' fees. It is therefore planned that the facility will be self-supporting.

The benefits to the city of Nelson from this project are significant. The facility adds to Nelson's tourism-heritage infrastructure providing the ability to draw tourists to the area and will retain those that have come to Nelson for other reasons. An operational streetcar running along the lakeside on an attractive route will focus attention on Nelson's waterfront and will likely inspire investor confidence in the development of the waterfront area. The project will not only become an economic generator but will also restore another proud part of Nelson's colourful past.

Culham concluded with a request that council endorse both the operation of #23 along the Lakeside route as well as the Nelson Electric Tramway Society's efforts to obtain capital funding to construct the street railway line.[4]

The society commissioned a feasibility study by Urbanics Consultants of Vancouver, B.C.[5] Their report, released in June 1989, examined the extent of community support for the project, preferred routes, the economic impact on the community, and the costs of operation. The consultants concluded that the project enjoyed strong support in the community, was economi-

The restored Bank of Commerce building (now the Canadian Imperial Bank of Commerce) on Baker Street

The Bank of Montreal building restored as part of the Baker Street project

145

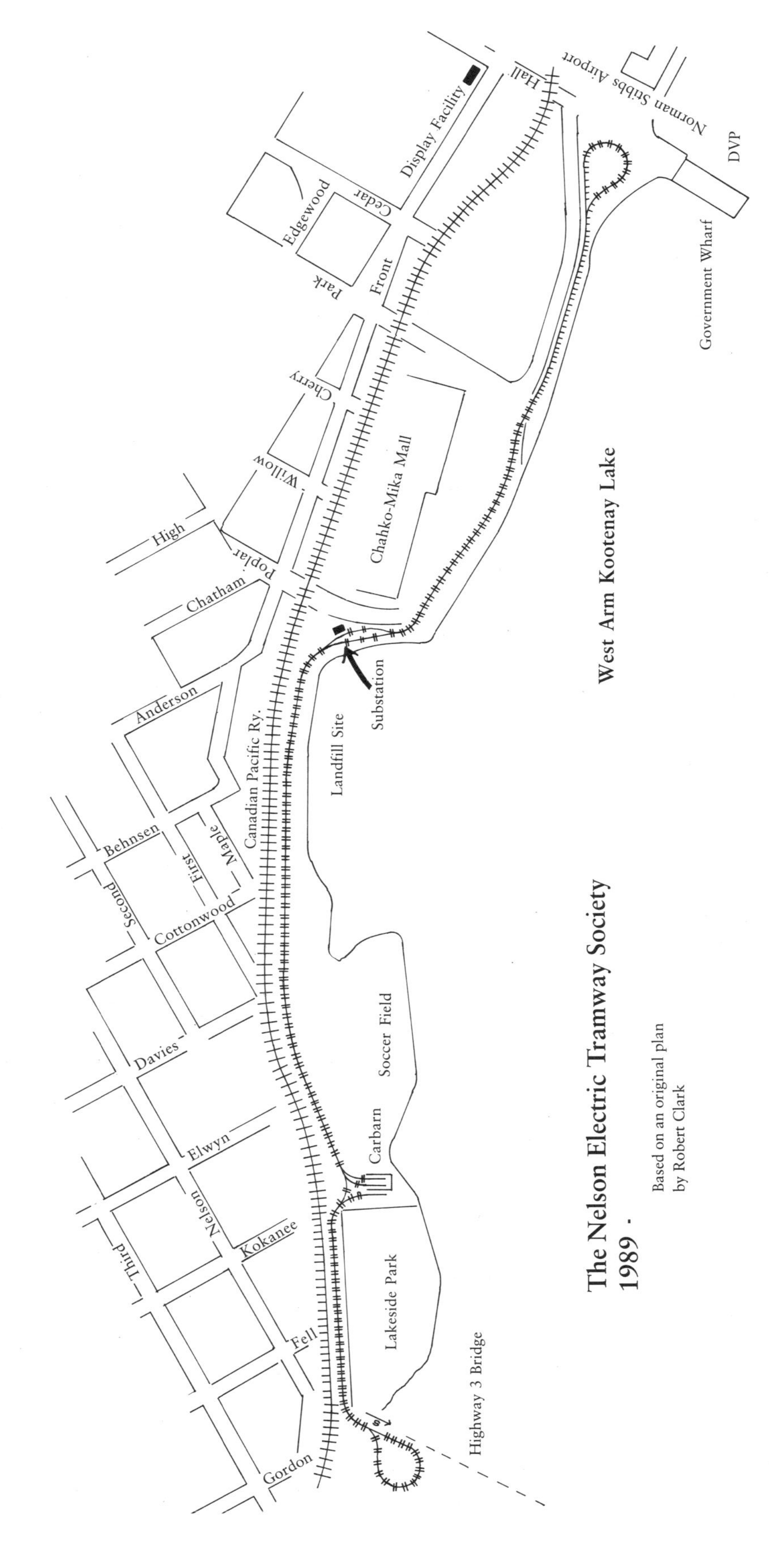

The Nelson Electric Tramway Society
1989 -

Based on an original plan
by Robert Clark

cally viable, and held the potential for significant economic benefits for the city.[6]

The proposed system would be constructed in two phases. In the first phase, the line would begin on the waterfront at the foot of Hall Street close to the downtown area, following the waterfront to Chahko-Mika Mall through whose parking lot it would pass, then run between the CPR tracks and the lake to Lakeside Park with a turning loop under the Highway Bridge which crosses the West Arm of Kootenay Lake, at the site where the streetcars once met the ferry.

The second phase would retrace to some extent the original pre-1950 line, at least along Baker Street. This part of the project, according to the consultants, might prove to be more difficult, since the CPR tracks had to be crossed as well as Highway 3A, to say nothing of the problems of operating a streetcar in automobile traffic in the downtown area.

The consultants concluded that, with all costs taken into account, and provided that a fare was charged for the streetcar ride, the line could be self-supporting.

The society intended to apply for a GO B.C. Program grant of $430,000 to finance part of the capital costs involved in building the line and approached the mayor and aldermen for support. Council, obviously influenced by the findings of the consultant's report, passed a motion on June 26 endorsing this application, despite the misgivings of some aldermen about aspects of the line's location.

On Wednesday, June 28, 1989, alderman W.H. Ramsden wrote to council describing his meeting with R.G. Adams the director of works and services and Mike Culham, and their subsequent tour of the proposed route. The major problem appeared to be finding a site for the carbarn.

Culham requested a site approximately three-quar-

Car 23 has just left the loop at the Government Wharf and is travelling along private right of way toward Chahko-Mika mall. The West Arm of Kootenay Lake is in the background.

ters of an acre in area preferably located very close to the city's ongoing landfill between the mall and the soccer field. After quite a bit of discussion, a possible site between the east end of the soccer field and the fenced nursery belonging to the park was proposed. This area also included the Chamber of Commerce logging competition site which would have to find another location.

Alderman Ramsden noted in the same communication that Howard Dirks, the local MLA, would announce on July 1 that the society would receive *GO B.C.* funding in the amount of $430,000 for the street railway project. He added that the society was anxious to begin work on the project once the information was released. In the meantime, the society received provincial approval to operate a street railway system in Nelson in the form of certificate #5400 issued "pursuant to the Railway Act."

Landfill projects are not noted for their aesthetic qualities. This was the point which Mayor Rotering stressed in a letter to council on July 2, 1989. Like many other North American cities, Nelson had a sister city in Japan, Shuzenji-cho. Mayor Rotering recommended that a small Japanese-style garden be developed as part of one of the streetcar stops, the whole area to be known as Shuzenji Station. His rationale was that the area concerned was largely landfill and in urgent need of beautification. Moreover, Nelson's sister city ". . . is nearing completion of an amazingly parallel miniature railroad development, albeit far more ambitious than ours. A major terminus in this [Shuzenji's] development will be known as Nelson Station . . ."[7] The matter was referred to council's parks committee. The city continued to add fill to the site throughout 1992.

The proposed line would pass through Chahko-Mika Mall's parking lot. The society preferred a route along the waterfront edge of the mall instead of following the vehicle-access road through the centre of the parking area. The waterfront route would solve problems of traffic congestion in the centre of the mall parking lot, while providing the most scenic view of the lake. Unfortunately, this approach would eliminate an unacceptable number of parking spaces. The management of the mall, while supporting the project in principle, preferred to see the street railway follow the vehicle-access road, the route ultimately chosen.[8]

The society envisaged a covered station platform to be located on the mall. In a letter to the mall's management, Peter Lee, the society's treasurer, solicited their input into its location and suggested that its development and construction might be a worthwhile project for mall merchants who undoubtedly would benefit from business generated by the new street railway.[9] In the same letter Lee provided some details about the proposed specifications for the line, at least as far as the mall was concerned.

The Streetcar System itself is intended to operate on standard gauge track over a total distance of 4,700 feet commencing at the foot of Hall Street and running along the waterfront, terminating at the rear of the concession stand at Lakeside Park [not as actually built]. The system will be powered by a 600V direct current using 2/0 grooved copper wire. Power poles are to be erected at 75 foot intervals at a height of 24 feet. Pole placements shall be 6 feet off track center and located on the boulevard next to existing curbing.

A total of 12 feet of operating space is required to accommodate trackage and poles. The track itself will be inlaid [i.e., set in the pavement instead of on top of it] and will therefore permit vehicular traffic to operate on the road similar to existing streetcar operations.

The building of a street railway of any size is a massive undertaking, and Nelson was fortunate at this time to obtain the services of Robert R. (Bob) Clark as Project Manager. Clark, who started with the Glasgow Tramways, had built the street railway in Fort Edmonton Park (an historical park located in Edmonton, Alberta). He had been heavily involved in the planning and development of the light rail transit (LRT) system in Edmonton as Edmonton Transit's light rail supervisor, and later took on the duties of director of operations for the Skytrain project in Vancouver. Clark took over his new responsibilities on October 1, 1989. Until the streetcar barn was sufficiently complete to permit

Proposed tramway theme restaurant

150

Tramway station at Chahko-Mika
mall

Robert R. (Bob) Clark

the project to be housed there, he was given office space on the third floor of City Hall.

One of his first tasks was to prepare a presentation for council describing the proposed line in detail.[10] The description he provided begins at the Government Wharf and follows the line to Lakeside Park.

The Government Wharf Area

The turning loop at the south end of the line would be built in the Government Wharf area. On the water side of the loop, the Water's Edge Marine Limited planned to build a hotel and restaurant incorporating the tramway station. As the proposal describes this facility, "The plan shows a fairly elaborate station which would tie into the Water's Edge Restaurant area by viewing windows and by a theme which could be carried into the building in the form of photos, murals, etc., so that the trams would be part of the background for diners, at the same time, allowing passengers to board and alight without interference between the two functions."

151

Unfortunately, neither the hotel nor the restaurant were built, and Clark's fall-back position, a simple turning loop, was constructed instead. From there the line would proceed north to Chahko-Mika Mall along a private right of way between the lake edge and the paved road leading into the mall.

Two other factors related to the Government Wharf loop required consideration. Its location was close to the end of the runway of Nelson's Norman Stibbs Airport - a location which later became a problem for the society. Secondly, it was essential to ensure that the street railway line could continue from the loop to the Baker Street area as part of Phase II of the project.

Chahko-Mika Mall

The line through Chahko-Mika Mall has already

Right-of-way between the park and the CPR track on the embankment

Passing track at the substation

been described. Great West Life, the proprietors of the mall, and the tramway society had discussed the possibility of constructing a station and loading platforms somewhere opposite the building's main entrance.

Chahko-Mika Mall to Carbarn

Where the line left the mall at its north end, it would descend a slight grade to a passing siding which would permit operation of two cars when equipment became available. This would also be the site of the line's substation, since it was closest to the main electrical feed from the city's 25 KV power line. From the passing siding, the line would turn again, and run between the landfill area on the water side and the CPR embankment on the city side until it reached the carbarn, located between the soccer field and Lakeside Park.

Carbarn

The carbarn, which was to be a replica of the 1910 structure, would shelter four cars and provide an inspection pit, a workshop, parts storage, washrooms, office, and trainmen's room. The CPR donated a caboose to be placed on this site as an interpretive centre and gift shop. When the new carbarn was built on the waterfront, it utilized virtually all of the materials from the old display

Carbarn under construction with Kootenay Lake's West Arm behind

facility. Recycling is taken seriously in the Kootenays.

Carbarn to the End of the Line

From the carbarn the track would follow the Lakeside Park service road between the CPR embankment and the park. At the north end of the line, Clark proposed three loop schemes. The first was the one chosen - a broad loop under the #3 highway bridge. Clark also urged that the attractive stone passenger shelter which figures in so many photographs of the original Nelson system be reproduced at this site.

The city's parks committee was not in favour of any of the proposed schemes for the loop at Lakeside Park. They proposed instead that the street railway terminate at the carbarn. Their rationale was that, "To proceed past this point would cause considerable problems with Parks vehicles, access control and pedestrian safety."[11] The committee's recommendation, had it been accepted, would have required backing of the car to turn it around. Such a practice in an area with considerable pedestrian traffic is one that street railway systems prefer to avoid.

In his response, Clark offered the following rationale for continuing the line past the carbarn.

Since the early conception of the lakefront tramway, it has been part of the plan that the line should service Lakeside Park and in fact should act as a 'people mover' to bring people into the park, thus helping to ameliorate problems associated with its operation. To terminate the tramway at the streetcar barn location would encourage patrons to park on Second Street and Kokanee and cross the CPR tracks on foot. Canadian Pacific is very much concerned at the present time about people trespassing on its property in this area and, in fact, have indicated that they would welcome the shift of focus which the tramway would provide. In the interests of good neighbourliness with the company and the safety of those concerned, this situation ought not to be encouraged.[12]

The CPR proved to be very generous to the proposed

154

street railway - in fact, a quarter of the streetcar line would be constructed on the railway's right of way .[13]

At a special meeting of council held on Monday, November 27, 1989, a resolution was passed that the tramway society not proceed with any construction in the Lakeside Park area until it had met with council.[14] Council had received erroneous information that the project was in jeopardy owing to its supply of rail drying up. When contacted, Clark stated this was most definitely not the case; he was still receiving offers of rail at reasonable prices. He also expressed his hope that determining the nature of the loop at Lakeside Park would not delay awarding of a permit to begin work on the carbarn, since it was imperative that the structure's foundation be poured before colder weather made this impossible. The society was willing to discuss the Lakeside

Car 23 on the main line approaching the platform at the carbarn

Park loop and the other outstanding problem (namely the provision of fill in the mall area) and since there seemed to be no problem in obtaining rail, council rescinded its motion of November 27 and granted a building permit for the carbarn.[15] Permission to build the Lakeside Park loop was finally obtained on February 23, 1990, subject to the society holding meetings to obtain public input.[16]

Community Contributions

In a letter to the author dated February 25, 1990, Culham was able to report some very encouraging progress.

We now have a commitment from CP Rail for all rail and ties, as well as all but one turnout . . . CP has also agreed to the lending of rail saws, track tools, benders etc. and have put together a crew of 12 volunteers to lay the complex trackage for us, such as the loops and the wye at the carbarn.

Most of the rail was salvaged from the abandoned CPR line from Rosebury to Nakusp.

In the Spring 1990 issue of the society's newsletter, Culham described the massive operation which the rail involved.

CP Rail volunteer Todd Dragland has amassed a crew of not less than 42 local CP employees who have begun laying track in earnest for us. Rails are all 85 lb. high-carbon steel; some 450 lengths have been donated, mostly all 39 feet long. These rails are stockpiled about a half hour's drive from the project site, and the first 80 lengths took two lowbed trucks and our hyab cranetruck one full day to move to the job site. Many thanks to Shoreline Trucking, their driver Charlie Bourgeois, Selkirk College's truck and instructor Neil Murdock, and to Bill Jones for operating the hyab and Bruce Meldrum [principal of Selkirk College] for operating the loader, which was donated by Maglio Industries. Truly a community-driven project! *

A project such as this involves many individuals and firms who contribute both time and money to its

* Modesty prevented two members of the society's executive (Mike Culham and Brian Freemantle) from mentioning their own role as as manual labourers on the project.

156

realization. Tramway society members Bill Kortegaard and Bill Jones spent many hours - the former in the machine shop at the carbarn, the latter as worker and supervisor during the barn's construction. Both became motormen when the line opened.[17] Electrician Bob Mowbray and fellow electricians from the International Brotherhood of Electrical Workers looked after the barn's electrical needs, while the A-3 Plumbing Company of Nelson contributed the plumbing installation.

City electrical inspector Clare Cornwell acted as technical advisor for the substation installation which was designed by his assistant, Mike Amos. (The building itself was designed by Bob Clark.) Volunteers from West Kootenay Power & Light Company led by Al Kraft installed the poles, while WKP&L's Les Westmacott wired the facility. Many other Nelson businesses and citizens donated money, materials and expertise.

Originally it had been suggested that trolley bus wire salvaged from Vancouver be used. Brian Kelly, a B.C. Transit official and a respected street railway historian, explained why this was not done. Trolley bus wire, once it is strung, acquires a *memory* for this configuration and cannot be adapted easily to a new site. R.G. Lingwood, B.C. Transit's general manager for Victoria

Car 23's interior looking toward the conductor's position at the back. Motorman Nora Clark tries out the wooden seats, while conductor Mike Culham mans the rear vestibule.

and small communities outside Vancouver, suggested that whatever overhead materials needed to be purchased would probably be obtained more cheaply if the society purchased them through B.C. Transit.[18] More significantly, the transit board indicated it might be willing at a future date to consider some financial assistance if the line were operated in conjunction with the Nelson Transit System.

In any project of this kind, publicity and fundraising are a major concern. In addition to the government funding obtained earlier, the society had raffled a 1920 Chevrolet donated by Bruce Meldrum, sold attractively-printed simulated bonds, and had been fortunate in obtaining the support of KBS radio and NRS Rosling Real Estate who generated financial and volunteer support. The two organizations collaborated on the bond drive; KBS provided daily information items on Nelson's street railway heritage, and under the direction of one of the society's directors, Ron Mack, carried out a pledge day which in twelve hours raised more than $17,000.[19] Finally, to keep Nelson residents in touch with the project, an information centre was located in Chahko-Mika Mall.

By July, a visitor to the area could begin to see that a street railway was, indeed, being built. Number 23 had been moved from the display facility at Front and Hall streets to the carbarn site on February 28, 1990. The shell of the new barn was complete, and considerable work had taken place on its interior. The loop at the highway bridge (Lakeside Park) was complete and the overhead poles in that area had been set in; rail had been laid part way from the carbarn to Lakeside Park. Rail and poles were in place beside the CPR embankment from the carbarn area to roughly the substation site. Some track had been laid in the carbarn area, while grading had been completed elsewhere.

There is more to a street railway than just the physical plant, however. To a casual observer, restoring a derelict streetcar body to its original appearance appears to be enormously complicated, which indeed it is. Unfortunately, unless the next stage - converting the body into an operating streetcar - takes place, the body will remain at the level of a static exhibit. A controller has to be rebuilt; obsolete air brake systems may have to be redesigned (if the original drawings are no longer available) and parts for the brake system either rebuilt or even manufactured; endless amounts of wire for lights, motors, the controller and the governor on the air brake system have to be installed, to say nothing of the mechanisms for operating the doors, steps and safety cradles. To quote Peter Cox, present operating superintendent of the Fort Edmonton line, "A minor miracle happens every time a carbody is transformed into an operating streetcar." It was fortunate for the Nelson system that Bob Clark came with the knowledge, ability, and contacts worldwide to do this.

Tracklaying in Pavement

It had always been anticipated that tracklaying through the paved surface in the mall area would be difficult. Construction here followed the practice used for city

Equipment used to string overhead wire

Society member Tony George and #23 beside overhead poles bearing aircraft warning markings

streets - the top of the rail would have to be flush with the paved surface. An excavation, 15 inches deep by 10 feet wide was cut through the pavement by volunteer city crews led by Dave Doman and Barrie Turner. Concrete slabs were laid over the ties to assist in future maintenance of the track. Unfortunately, once the excavation had been made, heavy rains slowed the work, as the area was repeatedly flooded and pumped dry throughout the summer. In the Lakeside Park area, the city had already planned to pave the roadway, so the society paid to have the crews pave between the rails as well.[20]

Completion of the System

The one hundred poles to support the overhead wire were set in place by a volunteer crew from the West Kootenay Power and Light Company led by Al Kraft. Wooden poles did not seem appropriate for the mall site, so metal poles were used. B.C. Transit supplied all overhead wire and many of the fittings at cost. Had the tramway society been obliged to order these components on its own, it might have faced a two-year delay.

Clark succeeded in obtaining two sets of trucks, compressors, and a Birney-type truck from the Société de transport intercommunales de Bruxelles (Brussels).

The shipment was a joint undertaking with the North Vancouver Museum and Archives who needed similar equipment for restoring British Columbia Electric Railway #153. The tramway society was not long in obtaining other equipment as well. Former BCER Birney car #400 arrived in September, 1990 on loan from the Royal British Columbia Museum. The frame of former Edmonton Radial Railway #52 was obtained with a view either to building a replica of one of the early cars (most likely of #21, given #22's history of accidents) or of an observation car.

For a time it looked as if all of the problems had been solved. Then, the Nelson Pilots Association raised serious objections to the power poles required on the Government Wharf loop near the end of the airport's main runway.[21] Transport Canada investigated the situation and concluded that the power poles were acceptable, thus removing perhaps the final barrier to completion of the line. To assist matters, the city painted the familiar orange and white warning stripes on those poles in line with the end of the runway and mounted red clearance lights on their tops.

Finally, all the rails had been laid, and on August 24, 1991, a last spike ceremony was held on the mall parking lot. For the occasion, #23 was towed down to

Last spike ceremony on the parking lot of Chahko-Mika mall, August 24, 1991. The speaker is Howard Dirks, MLA for the region. The car was towed to the mall since there was as yet no power.

the mall. Those who spoke on this occasion included Pastor Tom Wilkinson, Society President Bob Allen, Lyle Kristiansen, M.P., Mayor Robert Ramsden, Howard Dirks, M.L.A., and Bob Clark. Dirks and Ramsden drove the last spike.

A year of bad weather combined with two freak accidents to West Kootenay power lines prevented the anticipated completion of the overhead by volunteer crews. This work was contracted to the city of Nelson at cost, to be paid for by the society when it was able.

Eventually with the substation complete and wire strung as far as the carbarn, power was turned on to the overhead for the first time at 7:32 a.m. on Friday, April 3, 1992. At 11:00 a.m., the car's pole was put up, its interior lights came on, and at 3:00 p.m. after a few minor adjustments, the first streetcar to run in Nelson since 1949 made its initial trip. The car ran, in Clark's words, "as smooth as silk." It was driven about three quarters of the distance to the mall, but unfortunately, many of the flangeways both in the road crossings and on the mall had packed with dirt, and the rest of the day was spent clearing these out. Saturday morning was spent cleaning the remaining flangeways, checking the gauge, and making minor adjustments, after which the car was driven around the loop at the Government

The first streetcar in Nelson history to be parked on a mall parking lot, #23 waits for its crew who are having a lunch break at one of the mall's restaurants.

BCER Birney #400 on loan from the Royal British Columbia Museum

Wharf and back to the barn again. For about another hour, Mike Culham, Brian Freemantle, and Bob Allen, directors of the society, enjoyed the fruits of all their hard work as the car was driven up and down. Also on board were Nora Clark and Jan Culham.

Easter weekend, 1992 was particularly significant, since practical training of the operating crews was to take place. Prior to this Rollie Hurst, a retired CPR dispatcher, had taken the crews through the line's rule book, and Clark had introduced them to basic streetcar equipment. On Friday, Sheila White and Douglas Parker, editor and author, respectively, of this work and both volunteer motormen from the Edmonton Radial Railway Society at Fort Edmonton Park, arrived to begin the practical instruction. Parker had been Clark's assistant superintendent at the time the line in Fort Edmonton Park was opened and later became operating superintendent. White, in addition to her driving duties, works

Clearances are close under the highway bridge.

in the machine shop of the Radial Railway's carbarn. Her selection as the other member of the instructional team was not an accident, since two of the Nelson trainees were women, Nora Clark and Laurel Phillips. Eighteen trainees participated. The weekend also marked the first time that many mall patrons encountered a streetcar on the parking lot.

A particularly important event that Monday was a visit from Wilfred Hall, son of George Hall and brother of Les Hall (both superintendents of the earlier street railway). Wilfred Hall had also worked on the original system before going to work for the Post Office where he retired as postmaster for the city of Nelson and supervisor of post offices in the West Kootenay area.*

Following the Easter weekend's activities, the overhead wire was completed around the Lakeside Park loop under the highway bridge permitting crews to gain

*Hall recalls that his work with the system included greasing the track. Sometimes he was able to do this from a perch on the streetcar's safety fender, while his brother, Les, drove the car around the line. Other times he had to walk the length of the line. On occasion he also formed part of the sweeper's crew, operating the controls which activated the big brooms.

Private right-of-way beside the West Arm of Kootenay Lake. The highway bridge is in the distance.

additional experience driving an empty car back and forth without having to back up frequently as was the case on Easter weekend. On June 15 at 10:00 a.m., passenger service began, operating until 6:00 p.m.

Opening Day

The formal opening of the new street railway took place on July 1, 1992 as part of Nelson's Canada Day celebrations at Lakeside Park. Early that morning, #23 was taken down to the park and stationed there so that it would be readily visible to the happy throng who would later ride on it.

The day's festivities began with snowmobile [sic] racing across the West Arm of the lake, an event which attracted large crowds. In addition there was a delegation present from Nelson's sister city Shuzenji-cho. These visitors, along with various dignitaries, were #23's first passengers after the formal opening. The Royal Bank had commissioned a painting of the car which was displayed on the dais.* Wayne Germaine, president of the Chamber of Commerce, acted as master of ceremonies; Pastor Tom Wilkinson offered the invocation to open the festivities; Lyle Kristiansen, Member of Parliament for Kootenay West-Revelstoke, presented an award to a young Nelsonian; Cornelius (Corky) Evans, the member of the provincial legislature for Nelson-Creston, paid tribute to those who had been involved in #23's restoration; Howard Dirks,** formerly the MLA for the region spoke about the contribution which #23 represented, and Bob Allen, president of the Nelson Electric Tramway Society paid special tribute to Mike Culham, past-president, and to Bob Clark, project manager, for their efforts in bringing the project to a successful conclusion. The contribution of the late Lyle Ward was also remembered.

Finally, the Japanese delegation and the platform speakers boarded #23 which stood on the turning loop at the side of the park, and at 11:15 a.m., project manager Bob Clark, with society president Bob Allen

*The artist is Rick Slingerland, a former Nelson resident.

**This is probably an appropriate time to stress the major contribution made to this project by Howard Dirks whom we met earlier as the alderman who tried to rescue #23. Dirk's interest in the project continued as he became president and past president of the Nelson & District Chamber of Commerce. He was closely involved with the Chamber's committee which actively pursued the goal of returning streetcar operation to Nelson. Later as MLA for the Nelson area he was able to provide considerable support at the Provincial level as the project achieved fruition. Consequently, when the line opened on July 1, 1992, it was particularly appropriate that he should be one of the platform speakers.

Car 23 waits beside the highway bridge
for the formal opening of the line

OPENING DAY, July 1, 1992
- Lakeside Park

Howard Dirks flanked by the painting of
#23 commissioned by the Royal Bank

Car 23 driven by project manager
Bob Clark breaks the ribbon held by
Nelson Electric Tramway Society vice-
president Peter Lee (left) and past-
president Michael Culham (right).
Treasurer Brian Freemantle (in uniform) watches for oncoming automobiles, since the car is travelling the
wrong way around the loop on this
occasion only.

acting as conductor, drove #23 through a ribbon held by past-president Michael Culham and vice-president Peter Lee. The car stopped at the carbarn where the visitors disembarked to view the facilities and to enjoy a piece of the cake baked for the occasion. On their return to Lakeside Park, the line was opened to the public. During the day over 800 passengers were carried. Nelson's transit system offered free service to the park from the downtown area with tramway society member Rollie Hurst at the wheel of the bus.

Daily operation on the system continued until the car was withdrawn from service on Labour Day, by which time more than 20,000 passengers had been carried.

Streetcars had finally returned to the Kootenays!

A smiling Bob Clark turns #23 over to the regular crew immediately after the formal opening of the line

Nelson Electric Tramway Society

PHASE TWO

based on an original map by Robert Clark

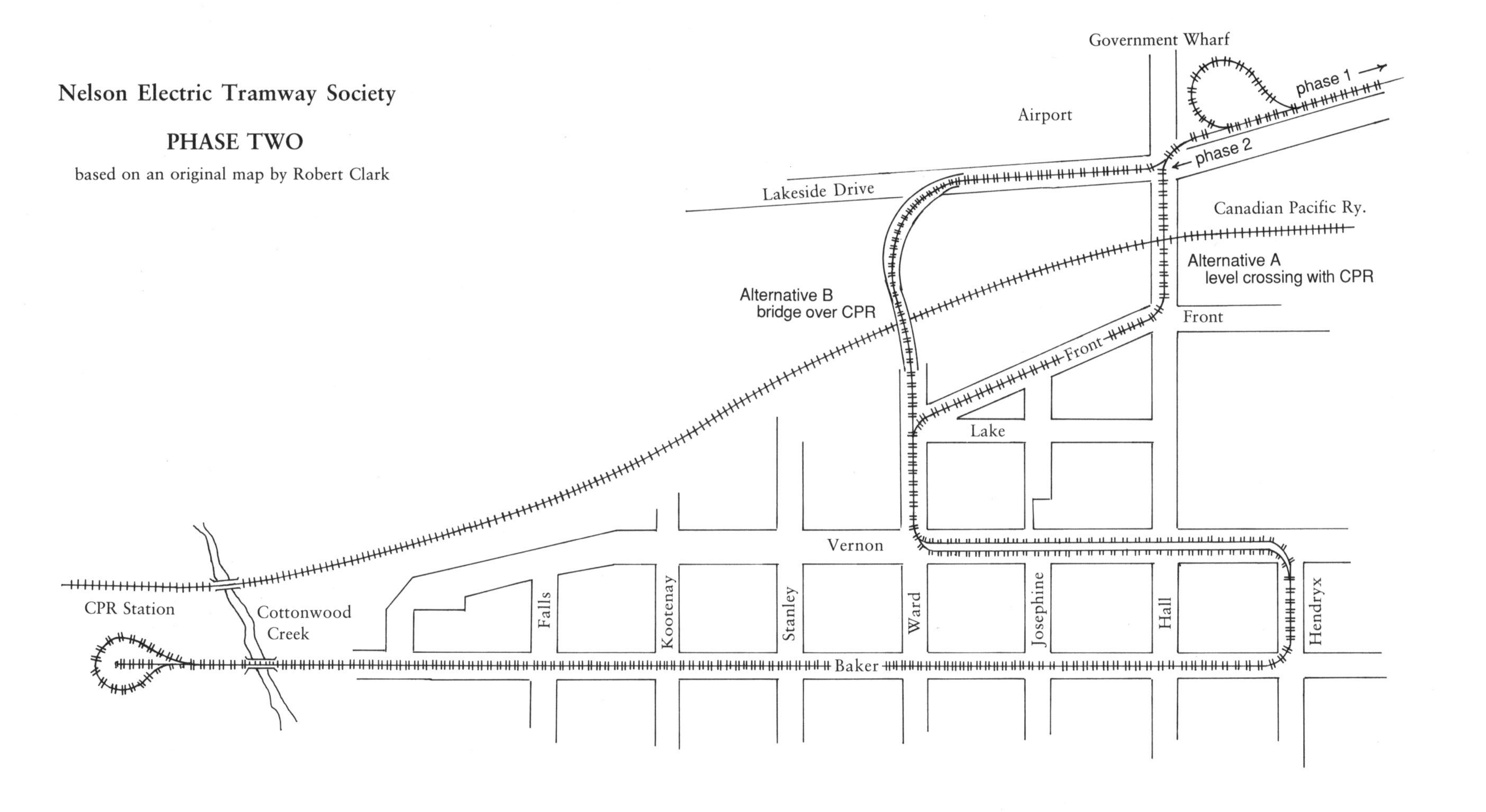

Epilogue

While work on the new street railway system was still in its early stages, thought was being given to Phase Two of the project. As mentioned in the previous chapter, the concept of operating in the business area of the city in fact preceded the idea of integrating the street railway into plans for the lakefront area. Peter Lee, tramway society vice-president, described the proposed extension.

To a considerable extent this follows the route of the former streetcar system on Front Street, Ward Street and

Baker Street showing restored buildings. In Phase Two this street would once again see streetcars.

Vernon Street but instead of turning up Josephine Street it continues a further two blocks to Hendryx Street to serve the Civic Centre (as had once been proposed for the old system) and an extra two blocks of Baker Street. Instead of turning up Stanley Street it would continue on Baker to the CPR Station (as was the case in 1901) where a turning loop would be installed. In addition to the above, the plan shows double track in Vernon Street flanking the grass median, forming in effect a long passing siding [the original line used Josephine Street for this purpose].*

In order to link with Phase I a connection is shown across the CPR tracks at Hall Street, and an allowance has been made in the estimate for this purpose. However it would be preferable, and more acceptable to the CPR, to install an overpass and this is shown as an alternative at Ward Street. If this were confined to a tramway, pedestrian and cycle bridge using standard pre-fabricated beams, the cost would be in the neighborhood of $500,000 in addition to the original estimate, for a total of $2.975 million or about $360 per foot of track.

It should be noted that a large proportion of the cost will be spent locally, as has been the case with Phase I of the tramway project and that there is a possibility of spin-off projects in the shape of improved methods of track and overhead construction which can be used on the new L.R.T. systems which are springing up in answer to concerns about the environment.

With the completion of Phase II the tramway would cease to be primarily a seasonally-operated tourist line and take its place as a practical line between downtown Nelson and the Chahko-Mika Mall to the benefit of both. The existence of a transit line along virtually the entire length of Baker Street would also encourage the extension of viable business locations beyond the present quite sharply defined limits. As part of the Nelson Transit System the line would become eligible for subsidy from transit tax funds.[22]

Appendix One

PERSONNEL

ADMINISTRATIVE STAFFS

Nelson Electric Tramway Company   1898-1908

Directors representing the parent company in London:
Charles S. Drummond
E. Garcke

Local Directors:

Francis W. Peters	President	1899- 1900
H.E. Croasdaile	President	1900-1908
Thomas J. Duncan	Vice-President	1899-1900
T.C. Duncan	Secretary-Treas.	1899-1900
J. Laingstocks	Director	
W.A. MacDonald	Director	
W.F. Mawdsley	Secretary	
M.F. Carey	Electrical Engineer and Manager	1899-1900
Archibald V. Mason	Secretary and General Manager	1901-1904
J. McPhee		1904

Offices located in the MacDonald Block

City Operation   1905-1908

T. Weekes	Manager	1905-1908
F.A. Smith	Electrical Supt.	1907

Nelson Street Railway Company   1909-1913

W.G. Morris	President	
G.W. McBride	Vice-President	
E.B. McDermid	Secretary-Treasurer	
H.E. Douglas	Secretary	1910
F.G. Poulton	Manager	1910

Nelson Street Railway Company
Nelson Street Railway   1913- 1949

Appleyard, C.W. — Secretary — 1914

Frank C. Ingram — Superintendent — 1910-1924

Ingram began as a motorman and conductor with the Nelson Electric Tramway Company, 1901-1905. He was appointed Superintendent in 1910.

George W. Hall — Superintendent — 1924-1932

George Hall began as a motorman in 1906. He retired in 1932 owing to ill health.

A.C. (Les) Hall — Superintendent — 1932-1949

(son of G.W. Hall) Les Hall began in 1914 after school hours helping in the barn and greasing the track. He was officially hired by the Nelson Street Railway on March 12, 1921 and worked as repairman, conductor, and motorman prior to his promotion to Superintendent in 1932.

Nelson Electric Tramway Society   1989-

Robert R. Clark — Project Manager — 1989
Superintendent — 1992-

Clark was hired as Project Manager for the line (October 1, 1989). On its completion, he was appointed General Superintendent.

OPERATING AND MAINTENANCE STAFF

The list provided below was compiled from several sources: Nelson city directories, newspaper accounts, George Hall's Timebook, Les Hall's Timebook, correspondence, old photographs and other sources. It was compiled initially by Clara Sutherland and the late Lyle Ward. Additions were made to it by David May and the author. While each of those who has worked on it has tried to make it as complete and as accurate as possible, it is unfortunately possible that someone who at one time or another worked on the street railway may inadvertently have been omitted. The author would be most grateful for additional information which could be included in any future listing.

Note: The dates given are those for which documentation has been found. They are not meant to be interpreted as the only date(s) on which the person named worked for the street railway involved, but rather, that as of that date he was employed by the system in that capacity according to the best evidence available.

(in alphabetical order)

Albion, J. T., motorman, 1910
Arnold, H. D., conductor, 1910
Bachynski, Ed, conductor
Barrett, J., 1910
Bellis, Harold B., conductor 1920
Bennecke, H. W., carbarn foreman, circa. 1908
Blakey, Francis L. (Lou), swingman, 1943; conductor, 1944-49
Brown, R. A., 1910
Bunce, Charles, maintenance and spare, 1943-49
Bunce, D. C. maintenance. 1935
Bush, Thomas, conductor, 1920
Cain, Harry, 1910
Campion, William R., conductor, 1899-1901
Canfield, Roy, motorman, 1945
Carmichael, Fred, 1949
Cartwright, Bill, motorman, 1946-49
Caruk, N., track and maintenance, 1949
Chapman, D., 1910
Clark, P. J., conductor, 1905
Couch, Sam, 1942
Coyle, motorman, December 1907
Dalrymple, Fred H., motorman, 1920-30
Dawson, Jim, conductor, 1939
Dingwall, Alec, swingman 1943, conductor, 1944-49
Dolphin, T., conductor, 1920
Dunn, Charles, motorman, 1901
Eliason, J., track and maintenance, 1949
Field, W. J., track and maintenance, 1949
Fletcher, George A., motorman, 1916-35
Franklin, G. W., conductor, 1910
Freed, motorman, 1910-14 (track foreman, 1911)

Francella, J., track and maintenance, 1949
Gillette, E., track and maintenance, 1949
Gobey, Leonard G., motorman, 1901-11
Grant, Alex, track and maintenance, 1901
Hall, A. C. (Les), started 1914; motorman 1929; Superintendent, 1932-49
Hall, George W., motorman, 1906-08, 1910-23; Superintendent, 1924-32
Hall, Lee, swingman 1943, motorman 1944-49
Hall, Wilfred, 1920-22 maintenance
Harlow, Ken, spare, motorman, trackman, 1947-49
Hawkins, J., conductor, 1899-1905
Hebden, A., motorman
Hinett, H., track and maintenance, 1936
Holland, C., motorman, 1949
Ingram, Frank C., motorman-conductor 1901-05, superintendent, 1910-24
Ingram, Jack, conductor, 1914
Jackman, Ed., conductor, 1910?-39
Jackson, H. D., conductor, 1905
Johnston, carbarn foreman, June 1907
Jordan, B. H., 1910
Joy, Jim, motorman, 1920-35
Kemping, 1910
Kyle, Joseph, motorman, 1901
Langille, E. F.., motorman, conductor, 1928-35
Langford, Horace A., 1900-01
Leicester, conductor, 1899
Lemmon, John H., conductor, 1928-37
Leslie, Bill, motorman, 1945-49
MacGregor, Elwood, maintenance, early 1930s
Manhart, G. H., lineman-motorman, 1900-11
Manson, Alfred E., motorman, 1942-49
Marshall, John Robert, conductor, 1919-29,
McCandlish, William Edward. (Scotty), conductor, 1938 -49
McDonnough, conductor, 1948
McInnis, S., track and maintenance, 1949
McKenzie, conductor, 1907
McKeown, R. G., 1920-31
Monro, Alec
Moore, Austin, motorman, 1944-49
Parrott, motorman, 1905
Peters, M. T., motorman, 1899
Phillips, D. conductor 1910
Pullen, Frank, assistant superintendent
Robert, O., track and maintenance, 1949
Robison, Jack, motorman, track and maintenance, 1932-49

Rowley, A. V. (Bert), conductor, 1931-
Ryan, Jack, conductor, 1939
Vulcano, Angelo, track and maintenance, 1933
Wallace, John
Warner, Norman, motorman, 1946-49
Webster, David, motorman-conductor,
  1937-49

Weekes, Thomas, foreman, motorman, and
  electrician, 1903-07
Wilson, E. , conductor 1899
Wools, W. A., motorman, 1920
Welsh, J. A., 1910
Zetnuk, Mike, track and maintenance
Zodewski, R., track and maintenance, 1949

Car 23 and Nelson Street Railway staff at Lakeside Park shortly after the Second World War.

From left to right: Superintendent A.C. (Les) Hall, Alfred Manson, David Webster, W.E. (Scotty) McCandlish, Alec Dingwall, Lee Hall, Lou Blakey, Roy Canfield, Bill Cartwright, Bill Leslie, Jack Robison, Charlie Bunce.

For a similar photograph taken in 1935, see page 100.

Appendix Two

EQUIPMENT ROSTER

NELSON ELECTRIC TRAMWAY COMPANY

Car Number(s)	Built	Builder
1, 2	1899	Canadian General Electric

Comments

Ordered August 10 1899, CGE orders c5459,
5460, 5461, E/N 724
21' closed cars, double truck, double end. Four, 40 h.p. motors.
Painted "claret red picked out with vermilion"

One car was sold "to the coast" or otherwise disposed of in May, 1902, leaving Nelson on May 27 (*NDN,* May 28, 1902). Since there are references to the "big open car" (i.e., #3) still running in Nelson at later dates, it is difficult to tell whether it was #1 or #2 that was shipped. Its receipt is acknowledged in a letter written by Austin Goward, the Victoria manager of the B.C. Electric Railway who also wished to know when the second car would be arriving. The only clue as to *which* car is contained in an item in the *Railway and Shipping World* in 1905 which states that "The B.C. Electric Ry. has purchased the first car owned by the Nelson Electric Tramway Co., and after overhauling it will be used on a branch." This may be any one of the 3 cars, but the term *first car* may be significant.

| **3** | 1900 | Canadian General Electric |

Comments .

Ordered Nov 7, 1899* CGE Order No. 5789, E/N 777
In fact , the car supplied was a Duplex Car built by Briggs Carriage
Works, Amesbury, Massachusetts. The car was supplied either as
a second hand car with CGE acting as brokers, or the order was
turned over to Briggs.

Open car, (est. to be 28') double truck, double end, convertible.
Painted yellow. Possibly GE 1000 motors. Brill 27G trucks. The
evidence suggests that it was destroyed in the carbarn fire in 1908.

| **4?*** | 1899 | Canadian General Electric |

Comments

Brian Kelly suggests that this car was British Columbia Electric
Railway's #44. The car was a closed, ST, DE, 21'6" vehicle. Its
truck was built by the Canadian Switch and Spring Co. The *NDN*
for December 3, 1904 says that the new car arrived in Nelson
yesterday "from the coast." It was described as a 16-18 passenger
car "and is being fitted for service in Nelson." It was probably the
second car burned in the 1908 fire.

* Despite the number 4, above, no evidence exists as to the actual
number assigned to the car on its arrival in Nelson.

NELSON STREET RAILWAY COMPANY
and NELSON STREET RAILWAY

Car Number(s)	Built	Builder
1, 2	1910	Ottawa Car Co. See drawing, page 74.

Comments

Double truck, double end, railway coach roof. Four 40 h.p. Allis-
Chalmers motors.Thirty inch wheels supplied with 2 1/8" tread,
but changed almost immediately to 3 1/2" tread. Gearing 69 to 15,
double reversible seats, fare registers, and electric passenger signal-
ling. Hand sanders. Providence fenders. Initially supplied with
hand brakes only, later equipped with Westinghouse air brakes
and sanders.

#1 renumbered 21; #2 renumbered 22 in 1933-34.

Converted to arch roof beginning with 22 (ex #2)
December 30, 1942. Originally painted olive (moss) green
and cream. Painted red and cream in 1925.

Bodies used on north shore as cottage and workshop, later
destroyed

| 3 | 1906 | Stephenson Car Co. |

Comments

Double truck, single end, deck roof.

Purchased second hand in 1924 from the Cleveland Railway
Company. Originally Forest City Railway's DE car # 3334. When
the Forest City Railway was absorbed in 1908, car was renumbered as #934 in Cleveland's 926-950 series. Rebuilt as a
single-end car. Brill 27G trucks, 4 GE 80 motors. GE K-28B
controller. Car was numbered 3 on arrival; renumbered 23 in
1933-34. Fitted with A&B type fender.

Body used as kennel, later as a craft shop on north shore. The car
has now been restored and is operated by the Nelson Electric
Tramway Society.

Sweeper (not numbered)   1911   Ottawa Car Co.

Comments

Single truck, double end. Brill truck. Allis Chalmers motors and
control equipment.

The sweeper may have been acquired second hand in which case
it was probably built about 1907. Retained the original olive
(moss) green colour scheme even after the streetcars were changed
to red and cream.

The body was used at a camp on the Ymir road and later was
burned.

23   restored and in operation 1992

Comments

Ex- Nelson Street Railway 23. Brill 84E trucks, 4 - 50 h.p. motors
K-35 controller, self-lapping brake

400   1922   Preston Car & Coach

Comments

Restored British Columbia Electric Railway #400. Birney. Four
wheels, double end safety car. On loan to the Society from the
Royal British Columbia Museum in Victoria.

4504   1951   Canadian Car & Foundry/
                                      St. Louis Car Co.

Comments

PCC all-electric. Obtained from the Toronto Transit Commission.
Brought to Nelson with the intention of using it for parts for #23,
a plan which was subsequently abandoned. The car's trucks were
traded to the Edmonton Radial Railway Society for a Preston
frame and electrical and mechanical equipment for #23.

BRITISH ELECTRIC TRACTION COMPANY
INVESTMENTS AS AT MARCH 31, 1901

NAME OF COMPANY

B.E.T. (Pioneer) Co., Ltd.
Bideford, Westward Ho! & Appledore Railway Co.
Birkdale & Southport Tramways Company, Ltd.
Birmingham & Midland Tramways, Ltd.
Brighton & Shoreham Tramways Co., Ltd.
British Thomson-Houston Co., Ltd.
Brush Electrical Engineering Company, Ltd.
Buenos Ayres & Belgrano Tramways, Co., Ltd.
City of Carlisle Electric Tramways Co., Ltd.
Cork Electric Tramways & Lighting Co., Ltd.
Dudley, Stourbridge & District Electric Traction Co.
Electrical Power Distribution Co., Ltd.
Gateshead & District Tramways Co.
Hartlepool Electric Tramways Co., Ltd.
Immisch Electric Launch Co., Ltd.
Kidderminster & District Electric Lighting & Traction Co., Ltd.
Leicester Tramways Co.
McKirdy & McMillan, Ltd.
Mumbles Railway & Pier Co.
Nelson Electric Tramway Co.
Oldham, Ashton & Hyde Electric Tramway, Ltd.
Poole & District Electric Traction Co., Ltd.
Potteries Electric Traction Co., Ltd.
Rossendale Valley Tramways Co.
Rothesay Tramways Co., Ltd.
South Shields Tramway & Carriage Co., Ltd.
South Staffordshire Tramways Co., Ltd.
  South Staffordshire Tramways (Lessee)

Southport Tramways Co., Ltd.
Swansea Improvements & Tramways Co.
Tramways & Light Railways Estates Co., Ltd.
Tynemouth & District Electric Traction Co., Ltd.
Weston-super-Mare, Clevedon & Portishead Tramways Co.
Wigan & District Tramways Co., Ltd.
Worcester Tramways, Ltd.
Yarmouth & Gorleston Tramways Co., Ltd.

NOTES

Chapter One

1 Charles St. Barbe, *First History of Nelson, B.C., With Sketches of Some of Its Prominent Citizens* (Nelson, B.C.: C.A. Rohrabacher, 1897), 2.

2 Tom Collins, "History What is History," in St. Barbe, *First History of Nelson*, 8.

3 Charles St. Barbe, *First History of Nelson, B.C.*, 8.

4 David Kay, ed., *Come With Me to Yesterday: Tales Retold of Pioneer Days in East Kootenay* (Cranbrook, B.C.: D.A. MacDonald and David Kay, 1965), 25.

5 Edward L. Affleck, ed., *Kootenay Lake Chronicles* (Vancouver, B. C.: Alexander Nicholls, 1978), 4:13-14.

6 Collins, in St. Barbe, *First History of Nelson*, 10.

7 David Scott and Edna H. Hanic, *Nelson: Queen City of the Kootenays* (Vancouver, B.C.: Mitchell, 1972), 43.

8 Collins, in St. Barbe, *First History of Nelson*, 10.

Chapter Two

1 Edward L. Affleck, "A Street Railway System for Nelson - Phase One," (1990), 1.

2 Kaye, *Come With Me to Yesterday*, 33.

3 Edward L. Affleck, *Sternwheelers Sandbars and Switchbacks* (Vancouver, B.C.: Alexander Nicholls, 1973), 58.

4 54 Vict., Cap. 70, 20 April, 1891.

5 17 Geo. V, Cap. 55.

6 55 Vict., Cap. 53, 23 April, 1892.

7 Edward L. Affleck, "Headstrong Houston and Hydro-Electric

Power" (1992).

8 Affleck, "A Street Railway for Nelson - Phase One," (1990),1.

9 57 Vict., Cap. 59, 11 April, 1894.

10 St. Barbe, *First History of Nelson*, 5.

Chapter Three

1 Margaret Ormsby, *British Columbia: a History* (Toronto: Macmillan, 1958), 315.

2 Nelson City Council, minutes, 12 July, 1898.

3 *The Miner*, 20 September, 1899.

4 Nelson City Council, minutes, 12 July, 1898.

5 Nelson City Council, minutes, 24 April, 1899.

6 Affleck, "A Street Railway System for Nelson - Phase One," (1990), 4.

7 "Section 3. Single cash fares are not to be more than ten (10) cents each, and fares on any cars operated after 11 p.m. are not to be more than double the ordinary maximum single fare. A class of tickets must be sold at not less than twelve (12) for one ($1) dollar. School children are to have the right to buy tickets at the rate not exceeding six (6) for twenty-five (25) cents, to be used only on school days between the hours of eight a.m. and five p.m. A ticket shall be deemed a fare. A class of tickets must be sold to bona fide workmen at the rate of twenty (20) for one dollar, the same to be used only by work men when travelling on the cars between the time the cars commence running in the morning and eight a.m. and between 6 p.m. and 7:30 p.m., such tickets to be sold only at the offices of the company within the City of Nelson, to bona fide workmen, who must state their names and occupations, and comply with other reasonable conditions. The classes of tickets above named, except workmen's tickets, shall be kept for sale on cars of the applicants at all times. In case of failure to supply such tickets for purchase by passengers, then said passengers shall be carried free until such tickets are provided."

Since those who drafted the By-law felt that other routes might be added in the future, the By-law also made provision for free transfers.

8 *The Miner*, 26 July, 1899.

9 *The Miner*, 1 August, 1899.

10 Ray Corley, letter to author, 24 January, 1962. "It might interest you to know that Canadian General Electric Co., between 1896 and up until approximately 1915 manufactured not only the electrical propulsion equipment for street railway cars, but also the cars themselves. In the early years, about 50% of the electrical equipment was supplied to other car builders, the balance going into cars of our own manufacture. As the years went on the car building operation gradually closed down here, even though the manufacture of the electrical propulsion equipment continued ... up to and including the present day."

11 Affleck, "A Street Railway System for Nelson - Phase One," (1990), 5.

12 55 Vict. Cap. 54, 23 April, 1892.

13 James Arthur Gilker, Charles H. Ink, John Houston, John McLeod, John Johnson, Thomas Madden, Wilmott Albert Crane, John Fred Hume, all of Nelson and Francis Stillman Barnard of Victoria.

14 Scott and Hanic, *Nelson*, p. 56.

15 Ibid., 66-68.

16 Affleck, "A Street Railway System for Nelson - Phase One," (1990), 5.

17 *The Miner*, 2 November, 1899.

18 *The Miner*, 22 November, 1899.

19 *Nelson Daily Miner*, 23 May, 1901. (*The Miner* became the *Nelson Daily Miner* on December 1, 1899.)

20 Douglas Parker, *No Horsecars in Paradise* (Toronto: Railfare, 1981), 128.

21 *Nelson Daily Miner*, 4 January, 1900.

22 Toronto City Council, minutes (1861), appendix, By-Law No.353, in Christopher Armstrong and H.V. Nelles *The Revenge of the Methodist Bicycle Company* (Toronto: Peter Martin, 1977), viii.

23 Christopher Armstrong and H.V. Nelles *The Revenge of the Methodist Bicycle Company*, 185.

24 Louis H. Pursley, *Street Railways of Toronto*, (Los Angeles: Interurbans, 1958), 142.

25 Parker, *No Horsecars in Paradise*, 35.

26 *Nelson Daily Miner*, 30 January, 1900.

27 Scott and Hanic, *Nelson*, 69.
28 Affleck, "A Street Railway System for Nelson-Phase One," (1990), 7.
29 *Nelson Daily Miner*, 24 March, 1900.
30 Canadian General Electric Company, order #5789, 7 November, 1899.
31 William D. Middleton, *The Time of the Trolley* (San Marino, CA.: Golden West, 1987), 225. 226.
32 Affleck, "A Street Railway System for Nelson - Phase One," (1990), 8.
33 Ibid.
34 Ibid., 10.
35 Ibid., 9.
36 *Nelson Daily Miner*, 10 November, 1900.
37 Affleck, "A Street Railway System for Nelson - Phase One," (1990), 9.
38 Ibid., 10-11.
39 Ibid., 8.
40 *Nelson Daily Miner*, 7/8 June, 1900.
41 Affleck, letter to author, 2 October, 1992.
42 Affleck, "A Street Railway System for Nelson - Phase One," (1990), 10.
43 Ibid., 11.
44 Affleck, letter to author, 2 October, 1992.
45 Government of Canada, *Fourth Census of Canada 1901,* (Ottawa: S.E. Dawson, Printer to the King's Most Excellent Majesty, 1902).
46 Affleck, letter to author, 27 August, 1990.
47 *Nelson Daily Miner*, 22 November, 1901.
48 *Nelson Daily News*, 28 May, 1901.
49 *Railway and Shipping World*, 1905.
50 Affleck, letter to author, 8 October, 1992.
51 Affleck, "A Street Railway System for Nelson - Phase One," (1990), 12.
52 Brian Kelly, letter to author, 21 November, 1992.
53 Affleck, letter to author, 27 August, 1990.
54 *Nelson Daily News*, 18 October, 1904.
55 J.H. Price, letter to Robert R. Clark, 21 February, 1990.
56 Affleck, "A Street Railway System for Nelson - Phase One," (1990), 13.
57 *Nelson Daily News*, 25 February, 1908.
58 Affleck, "A Street Railway System for Nelson - Phase One," (1990), 13.
59 Daily *Canadian (Nelson)*, 25 April, 1908.
60 D*aily Canadian (Nelson)*, 27 April, 1908.
61 *Nelson Daily News*, 8 October, 1909.

62 Affleck, "A Street Railway System for Nelson - Phase One," (1990), 15.

Chapter Four

1 Affleck, letter to author, 18 October, 1990.
2 Affleck, "The Granite-Poorman Platinum Rush" (1991).
3 Affleck, "A Street Railway System for Nelson - Phase Two," (1990), 1.
4 The proposed street railway's provisional directors included W.G. McMorris, R.L. Lennie, W. O. Rose, and G.W. McBride. *Nelson Daily Daily News*, 8 October, 1909.
5 *Nelson Daily News*, 8 September, 1908.
6 Affleck, "A Street Railway System for Nelson - Phase Two," (1990), 3.
7 Ibid., p.2
8 *Nelson Daily News*, 8 October, 1909.
9 Affleck, "A Street Railway System for Nelson - Phase Two," (1990), 2.
10 *Nelson Daily News*, 2 November, 1909.
11 Affleck, "A Street Railway System for Nelson - Phase Two," (1990), 2.
12 *Nelson Daily News*, 28 April, 1910.
13 *Nelson Daily News*, 12 July, 1910.
14 *Nelson Daily News*, 10 September, 1910.
15 *Nelson Daily News*, 19 June, 1910.
16 *Nelson Daily News*, 30 October, 1910.
17 *Nelson Daily News*, 28 April, 1910.
18 *Nelson Daily News*, 2 November, 1910.
19 *Nelson Daily News*, 3 November, 1910.
20 *Nelson Daily News*, 8 November, 1910.
21 *Nelson Daily News*, 29 December, 1910.
22 *Nelson Daily News*, 22 December, 1910.
23 *Nelson Daily News*, 22 March, 1911.
24 Affleck, "A Street Railway System for Nelson - Phase Two," (1990), 5.

Chapter Five

1 H.P. Thomas, Manager, Street Railway Department, letter to William Rae, Chief Inspector of Railways, 18 September, 1916.
2 Affleck. "A Street Railway System for Nelson - Phase Two,"(1990), 6.
3 Wilfred Hall. "Nelson Street Railway," Nelson Old Timers Banquet, 16 March, 1981.
4 Austin Moore. videotaped interview, n.d.

5 Rae, letter to Chief Engineer, Railway Department, Province of British Columbia, 7 March, 1919.
6 Rae, letter to Chief Engineer, 20 August, 1919.
7 Wilfred Hall, interview with author, 18 April, 1992.
8 D. S. Webster, videotaped interview, n.d.
9 Affleck, letter to author, 2 October, 1992.
10 Rae, letter to C.F. McHardy, Mayor, city of Nelson, 26 May, 1921.
11 Rae, letter to Chief Engineer, 26 May, 1921.
12 Affleck, "A Street Railway System for Nelson - Phase Two," (1990), 7.
13 Ibid., 8.
14 Affleck, letter to author, 30 November, 1972.
15 Affleck, letter to author, 30 July, 1990.
16 Affleck, letter to author, 2 October, 1992.
17 Ibid.
18 *Nelson Daily News*, 4 February, 1908.
19 Russell Potter, personal interview with author, n.d.
20 Affleck, "A Street Railway System for Nelson - Phase Two," (1990), 11.
21 Rae, letter to Deputy Minister, Dept. of Railways, 16 October 1942.
22 D. S. Webster, videotaped interview, n.d.
23 Rae, letter to Deputy Minister, Dept. of Railways, 16 October, 1942.
24 A.C. (Les) Hall, Superintendent, Nelson Street Railway, letter to Rae, 8 February, 1944.
25 Affleck, "A Street Railway System for Nelson - Phase Two," (1990), 5.
26 J.H. Short, Acting Chief Inspector, Dept. of Railways, letter to Deputy Minister, 30 July, 1945.
27 Affleck, "A Street Railway System for Nelson - Phase Two," (1990), 12.
28 Norman Gidney, jr., ed. "History of Nelson Transit," *The Commuter*, n.d.
29 Affleck, "A Street Railway System for Nelson - Phase Two," (1990), 12.
30 Claude R. Kingsbury, "Preliminary Estimate of Cost of Overhead for Installation of Trackless Trolley," 6 June, 1947.
31 Kingsbury, letter to Hall, 12 November, 1948.
32 A. C. (Les)Hall, letter to author, 8 September 1961.
33 in Gidney, "History of Nelson Transit," n.d.

Chapter Six

1 A. C. (Les) Hall, letter to author, 8 September 1961.
2 Marvin Singleton, letter to the Corporation of Nelson, 28 October, 1980.
3 Douglas P. Ormond, City Administrator, letter to Singleton, 7 November, 1980.
4 Ormond, letter to Singleton, 5 December, 1980.
5 Ormond, letter to Downtown Core Steering Committee, 27 March, 1981.
6 Wray F. Suffredine, Executive Director, Nelson Chamber of Commerce, letter to Mayor Louis Maglio and Council, 11 August, 1982.
7 *Nelson Daily News*, 26 August, 1982.
8 Arvid D. Schneider, letter to Ormond, 27 August, 1982.
9 Robert Adams, letter to Ormond, 16 September, 1982.
10 Nelson City Council, minutes, 1982, 634.
11 *Nelson Daily News* 23 September, 1982.
12 Lloyd Mosely, City Treasurer, letter to Ormond, 27 September, 1982.
13 Ormond, letter to Nelson Chamber of Commerce, 6 October, 1982.
14 Ward, letter to author, 9 February, 1983.
15 Streetcar #23 Committee, "Street Car #23," n.d.
16 Mosely, letter to Mayor and Council, 9 July, 1985.
17 D. Smithson, Alderman, letter to Mayor and Council, 10 February, 1986.
18 C.L. Olson, Deputy Clerk, letter to Nelson & District Chamber of Commerce, 20 February, 1986.
19 Ormond, letter to Nelson & District Chamber of Commerce, 25 February, 1986.
20 Douglas White, Tourism Development Manager, Economic and Regional Agreement, Canada/B.C., letter to Howard Dirks, 8 July, 1986.
21 Robert Brisco, letter to Howard Dirks, 30 July, 1986.
22 Stephanie Forsyth, President, Nelson & District Chamber of Commerce, letter to Mayor and Council, 6 February, 1987.
23 Ormond, letter to Nelson & District Chamber of Commerce, 21 July, 1987.
24 *Nelson Daily News*, 13 August, 1987.
25 Olson, letter to Dr. Michael Culham, Chairman, Streetcar #23 Committee, 16 October, 1987.

26 Allen Early, President, Nelson & District Chamber of Commerce, letter to Mayor Gerald Rotering, 28 January, 1988.

Chapter Seven

1 *Newsletter*, Nelson Electric Tramway Society (NETS), i(Fall, 1989), 1.
2 *Nelson Daily News*, 8 December, 1988.
3 Michael Culham, letter to City Council, 11 March, 1989.
4 Culham, letter to City Council, 13 March, 1989.
5 Urbanics Consultants Ltd., "Nelson Tramway Feasibility Study," June, 1989.
6 Nelson City Council, minutes, 26 June, 1989.
7 Gerald Rotering, Mayor, letter to Council, 2 July, 1989.
8 *Nelson Daily News*, 27 June, 1989.
9 Peter W. Lee, Treasurer (NETS), letter to Garth Walker, Manager, Chahko-Mika Mall, 18 September, 1989.
10 NETS, Presentation to City Council, 14 November, 1989.
11 W. Ramsden, Alderman, Chairman, Parks Comittee, letter to Council, 16 November, 1989.
12 Robert R. Clark, letter to Robert Adams, Director of Works and Services, 23 November, 1989.
13 Culham, letter to author, 25 February, 1990.
14 Ormond, letter to Mayor and Council, 30 November, 1989.
15 C.L. Olson, Deputy Clerk, letter to Culham, 13 December, 1989.
16 Olson, letter to Culham, 23 February, 1990.
17 *NETS Gazette*, iii (Spring 1990), 1.
18 R.G. Lingwood, letter to Culham, 10 October, 1989.
19 *NETS Gazette*, iii (Spring 1990), 1.
20 *NETS Gazette*, iii (Spring 1990), 1.
21 R. J. Thompson, Secretary, Nelson Pilots Association, letter to Adams, 26 September, 1990.
22 Lee, letter to Con Diamond, Chairman, Marketing Committee, Nelson & District Chamber of Commerce, 14 August, 1990.

PHOTOGRAPHIC CREDITS

The first number given is the page; the second is the catalogue number where one exists. Where only one number is given it is to be understood that it refers to the page only and that photographs from that source do not bear a catalogue number.

Every effort has been made to secure permission to use these photos from the copyright holder when such person(s) could be identified.

Allen, Robert
161

British Columbia Archives and Records Service (BCARS)
If ordering photographs from this source, the letters HP should be added to the numbers shown below, e.g. HP4213.

6:36918, 7:4213, 8:90359, 9:44524, 11:62970, 12:62970, 17:45901, 18:17872, 21:5257, 25:90332, 38:36933, 43:8937, 47:37640, 49:5231, 50:5245, 63:31699, 72:5250, 98:37761, 131:83295

B.C. Transit
29

Clark, Robert
148, 157, 160, back cover (upper right)

BIBLIOGRAPHY

Affleck, Edward L. Letters to author, 27 August 1990;
18 October 1990; 2 October, 1992; 8 October, 1992.

Affleck, Edward L. Letter to David Wilkie, 30 November
1972.

Affleck, Edward L. "The Granite-Poorman Platinum Rush."
1991 .

Affleck, Edward L. "Headstrong Houston and Hydro Electric Power." 1992.

Affleck, Edward L. "A Street Railway System for Nelson."
1990.

Affleck, Edward L. *Kootenay Lake Chronicles*. Vol. 4.
Vancouver, B.C.: Alexander Nicholls, 1978.

Affleck, Edward L. *Sternwheelers Sandbars and Switchbacks*. Vancouver, B.C.: Alexander Nicholls, 1973.

Armstrong, Christopher, and H.V. Nelles. *The Revenge of
the Methodist Bicycle Company*. Toronto: Peter Martin,
1977.

Basque, Garnet. *West Kootenay, the Pioneer Years*. Langley,
B.C.: Sunfire, 1990.

Canadian Railway and Marine World.

Collins, Tom. "History What is History." *Nelson Tribune,* 25 September,1897. (offers corrections to St. Barbe).

Corley, Ray. Letter to author, 24 January 1962.

Daily Canadian (Nelson)

Dorman, Robert. *A Statutory History of the Steam and Electric Railways of Canada 1836-1937.* Ottawa: Department of Transport, 1938.

Ewart, Henry. *The Story of the B.C. Electric Railway Company.* Vancouver, B.C.: Whitecap, 1986.

Gidney, Norman, jr. "History of Nelson Transit." *The Commuter* [an early B.C. Transit publication], n.d.

Graham, Clara. *Kootenay Mosaic.* Vancouver, B.C.: Evergreen, 1971.

Hall, A.C. (Les). Letters to author, 20 August 1961; 19 September 1961; 9 March 1967.

Hall, A.C. (Les). Superintendent's time book.

Hall, George. Superintendent's time book.

Hall, Minnie. Interview with author, 24 August, 1988.

Hall, Wilfred. Interview with author, 18 April, 1992.

Hall, Wilfred. Talk given at the Old Timers' Banquet, 16 March 1981. Nelson, B.C.

Kay, Dave, ed. *Come With Me to Yesterday. Tales Retold of Pioneer Days in East Kootenay.* Cranbrook, B.C.: D.A. MacDonald and Dave Kay, 1965.

Kelly, Brian. Letters to author, 18 June 1991; 21 November, 1992.

Lee, Helen. *The Silver King.* Nelson, B.C.: Kootenay Museum Association and Historical Society, 1986.

May, David. *Five Miles On a Nickel*. Nelson, B.C.:
The Author, 1988.

Middleton, William D. *The Time of the Trolley*. San Marino,
CA.: Golden West, 1987.

The Miner. (became *Nelson Daily Miner* 1 December 1899.)

Nelson Daily Miner.

Nelson Daily News.

Nelson City Council. Minute books.

NETS Gazette. (Nelson Electric Tramway Society newsletter.)

Ormsby, Margaret. *British Columbia: A History*. Toronto:
Macmillan, 1958.

Parker, Douglas V. *Nelson Street Railway*. Bulletin 3.
Victoria, B.C.: British Columbia Railway Historical Association, 1961.

Parker, Douglas V. *No Horsecars in Paradise*.
Toronto: Railfare, 1981.

Potter, Russell. Personal interview, n.d.

Price, J.H. Letter to Robert Clark, 21 February 1990.

Pursley, Louis H. *Street Railways of Toronto 1861-1921*.
Los Angeles CA.: Interurbans, 1958.

Rieger, Hal. *The Kettle Valley and Its Railways*. Edmonds,
Washington: Pacific Fast Mail, 1981.

St. Barbe, Charles. *First History of Nelson, B.C. With
Sketches of Some of Its Prominent Citizens*. Nelson, B.C.:
C.A. Rohrabacher, 1897.

Sanford, Barrie. *McCulloch's Wonder: The Story of the
Kettle Valley Railway*. Vancouver, B.C.: Whitecap, 1978.

Scott, David, and Edna H. Hanic. *Nelson: Queen City of the
Kootenays*. Vancouver, B.C.: Mitchell, 1972.

Smyth, Fred J. *Tales of the Kootenays.* North Vancouver, B.C.: J.J. Douglas, 1977.

Sutherland, Clara. Personal interview, 5 August, 1992.

Turnbull, Elsie G. *Ghost Towns and Drowned Towns of West Kootenay.* Surrey, B.C.: Heritage House, 1988.

Turner, Robert D. *Sternwheelers and Steam Tugs.* Victoria, B.C.: Sono Nis, 1984.

Ward, Lyle. Letter to author, 9 February 1983; 25 February, 1983; 13 January 1984; 21 June 1984.

INDEX